Lianne McTavish onstage in June 2011. Photo by David Ford.

Feminist Figure Girl

FEMINIST FIGURE GIRL

Look Hot
While You Fight
the Patriarchy

Lianne McTavish

Original cover image © Patrick J. Reed

Published by State University of New York Press, Albany

For information, contact State University of New York Press, Albany, NY
www.sunypress.edu

Production, Jenn Bennett
Marketing, Fran Keneston

Library of Congress Cataloging-in-Publication Data
McTavish, Lianne, 1967–
    Feminist figure girl : look hot while you fight the patriarchy / Lianne McTavish.
      pages cm
    Includes bibliographical references and index.
    ISBN 978-1-4384-5476-4 (pbk. : alk. paper) — ISBN 978-1-4384-5477-1 (hard-
    cover : alk. paper) — ISBN 978-1-4384-5478-8 (ebook) 1. Feminism—His-
    tory—21st century. 2. Feminism and sports. 3. Women bodybuilders. I. Title.
    HQ1155.M38 2015
    305.4209—dc23
                                                          2014008112

10 9 8 7 6 5 4 3 2 1

For my inspirational trainers:

Gillian Kovack (IFBB Pro Heavyweight Bodybuilder)

and Audrey Shepherd (Monster Girl Fitness, Inc.)

Contents

Images

Acknowledgments

Most of my research for the Feminist Figure Girl project took place at the gym, where I worked out with professional trainers and friends. Gillian Kovack, a heavyweight bodybuilder who won her IFBB Pro Card in 2011, taught me how to lift weights and guided me into the world of bodybuilding competitions. Without her friendship and intellectual engagement, this project would not have been possible. Audrey Shepherd trained me during the year leading up to my figure/bodybuilding competition, providing continual emotional support along with strenuous "leg days" that I won't soon forget. I received invaluable advice from my diet and posing coach, Raejha Douziech, an IFBB professional bodybuilder and figure athlete. Another central collaborator was Patrick J. Reed, a visual artist who designed the Feminist Figure Girl logo and posters and, more important, took photographs of all aspects of my research, from the meticulous food preparation to posing lessons and tanning rituals. I also appreciate the work of another designer, Jeffrey Klassen, who constructed and updated the Feminist Figure Girl blog site (feministfiguregirl.com). Many others have contributed to this blog over the years, particularly Deanna Harder, a certified trainer and figure competitor who continues to write the "Ask a Trainer" feature on my site. Others who have taken a special interest in Feminist Figure Girl and have written guest posts include Jody Bacso, Donica Belisle, Lorrie Egerter, Janis Finkelman, Dan Given, Ryan Hough, WhiteFeather Hunter, Kristen Hutchinson, Morris Lemire, Sasha Mullally, Anne Pratt, and Sarah Waurechen. The energetic staff at the World Health Club on Jasper Ave in Edmonton, where I now work part-time as a spin instructor, provided ongoing encouragement. I am grateful to manager Bob Langevin for allowing Patrick to photograph me working out at this gym on several occasions.

Although I did not seek external funding for this embodied research project, I did rely on the academic expertise of my colleagues at the University of Alberta. Anne Whitelaw, now at Concordia University, read and responded to multiple versions of every chapter of this book. The members of my writing group, Julie Rak, Liz Czach, and Amy Kaler, provided insightful commentary on some early chapters, while my queer studies reading group critiqued Chapter Four of the manuscript. Natalie Loveless, a talented colleague in the Department of Art and Design, asked me challenging questions that changed the shape of this book, and introduced me to the critical work of visual artist Heather Cassils. While everyone in my home department supported my research, I am especially thankful to Betsy Boone, Sean Caulfield, Lisa Claypool, Joan Greer, Liz Ingram, Bonnie Sadler-Takach, and Maria Whiteman. I have given scholarly talks about this work at the University of Alberta, and by invitation from Susan Amussen at the University of California, Merced. I thank Wade Kelly for asking me to present my ideas at both Nerd Nite Edmonton and the first Global Nerd Nite, held in Brooklyn in 2013. Parts of Chapter Two were previously published in the *Western Humanities Review*, and sections of Chapter Three appeared in *Topia: Canadian Journal of Canadian Studies*; I include that material here with permission. I must also recognize the contributions of Beth Bouloukos, the Acquisitions Editor at SUNY Press who realized and promoted the value of my manuscript, along with the anonymous external referees who offered insightful criticism of it.

Many friends and family members provided invaluable assistance, including Kelly-Jo Aldworth, Ryan Arcand, Sjoukje Bouma, Judy Burwell, Elaine Cardinal, Faith Cardinal, Janice Wright Cheney, Danielle Comeau, Peggy Cooke, Julian Forrest, Lisa Given, Nicole Glenn, Simone Leibovitch, Beverly Lemire, Lisa Prins, Glenda Turner, Steve Turner, Toccara Winterhawk, and all the readers of my blog. I owe, however, my greatest debt to Lee Spence, my long-suffering partner of twenty-seven years, who endures with good nature my maniacal bursts of energy. Finally, I can scarcely forget our future son who, though not yet born, is currently making his presence known as I embark on my next body project.

Introduction

Becoming Feminist Figure Girl

"We rise to the challenge of movement."
—Stacy Holman Jones[1]

It is December 12, 2009, and I am at the gym, feeling euphoric. I am pumping away on the elliptical machine with the resistance level set at sixteen and Nirvana's *Live at Reading* pounding in my ears. Since I have already completed an hour-long upper-body session with my personal trainer, my workout is almost done, but I don't want to leave. I close my eyes and savor the intense endorphin rush that washes over me. I am a forty-two-year-old woman who has achieved many goals—defending a doctoral thesis, writing books, and rising to the level of full professor by age thirty-nine. Yet none of them is as satisfying to me as building muscle and losing fat. What in the hell is going on here?

In this book I will attempt to answer this question as I consider why bodybuilding could be more rewarding than other professional or intellectual accomplishments. I devised the Feminist Figure Girl project, as well as a weekly blog (feministfiguregirl.com) after giving a guest lecture in a women's studies class at the University of Alberta. As a longtime reproductive rights activist, I had been asked to speak about the changing political strategies of the prochoice movement in Canada. The assigned reading was "The Cultural Production of Pregnancy: Bodies and Embodiment at a New Brunswick Abortion Clinic," an article I had published in 2008 about my experiences as a prochoice escort at Fredericton's Morgentaler Clinic.[2] In this article

I combined personal observation with research about health policy, feminist theory, and the politics of space to examine how every Tuesday morning, when appointments were held, the perimeter around the clinic became a performative staging area for prochoice activists and antiabortion protestors alike. The students were intrigued both by my descriptions of the front lines of the abortion debate and my reassessment of the medicalization of pregnancy. I wondered how to produce more scholarship that melded interdisciplinary research with first-hand, embodied experiences. Yet the activity that had occupied much of my time and energy since arriving in Edmonton in 2007 was weight lifting, a practice that seemed neither political nor feminist. It would be difficult to translate my daily workouts into research results.

After some brainstorming, I decided to challenge this assessment by training for a local figure competition to be held in the spring of 2011. I planned to engage in every activity necessary to succeed in the competition, from consistent dieting to eating meat, ingesting supplements, and tanning. All of this would be new to me. I guessed that it would take me well over a year to increase my muscle mass and lose most of my body fat. In addition to analyzing the physical transformation of my body in terms of feminist and visual theory, I would have to learn the proper posing techniques, practice walking in four-inch heels, whiten my teeth, grow my fingernails, and do something about my increasingly wrinkled face and sagging neck. Figure competitions are not exactly like the female bodybuilding contests made famous by such films as *Pumping Iron II: The Women* (1985).[3] Although figure contestants train similarly and are judged on the symmetry, proportion, and definition of their muscles, "excessive muscularity" is considered undesirable. Ideal competitors, colloquially known as figure girls, display shapely "feminine" forms, complete with small waists, curvaceous legs, and beautiful faces. Dressed in form-fitting bikinis, they are confident and poised while striking four standard, quarter-turn poses: from the front, they raise their shoulders, flare their backs, and lift their arms to frame their bodies in a strangely awkward manner; from each side, they curve one arm in front and one behind their bodies while pushing their buttocks outward; and from the back, they raise their shoulders and widen their upper bodies to enhance their already tiny waists. Unlike fitness contests, which require participants to demonstrate strength and flexibility, figure girls simply present themselves for the visual evaluation of an audience. Even as the judges scrutinize the condition of their bodies, they also rate the figure girls' hair, makeup, skin tone, and costume. In short, a figure competition is like a bodybuilding display and beauty pageant rolled into one.

At first I was frankly appalled by these competitions. Were figure contests designed to counteract the transgressive potential of female heavyweight bodybuilding? Did they offer token rewards to women who looked and acted like Barbie dolls, embracing their own objectification? I brought these concerns to my trainer, Gillian Kovack, thinking that as a competitive heavyweight bodybuilder she might dismiss figure contests, considering them inferior to her own ambitions (see Figure 1). A substantial amount of feminist theorizing about women's heavyweight bodybuilding would support such a reaction. Scholars including Barbara Brook and Chris Holmlund argue that the built female body both challenges assumptions about women's natural physical weakness and resists cultural norms of femininity.[4] Pamela L. Moore contends that when the female bodybuilder flexes her rippling chest muscles, revealing taut skin and pulsing veins, she dispels the longstanding association of women's bodies with mysterious interiority.[5] In contrast, figure girls seem to conform more rigidly to feminine ideals. Yet my trainer was unimpressed by my characterization of figure girls as beauty contestants, and insisted that they were serious athletes. Once I began to meet active figure girls I realized she was right. These women—especially Jennifer Flontek, both a cardio-kickboxing instructor at my gym and a figure champion with a ripped back, strong personality, and amazing amount of energy—came across as dedicated, disciplined, and admirable (see Figure 2). Hardly passive Barbie dolls, they made personal and professional sacrifices to reshape their bodies and work toward long-term goals that would be unattainable for most women.

I began to wonder if figure competitions could challenge gender roles as well as reinforce them, sending contradictory messages worth noting and maybe even worth experiencing. Figure girls spend hours in the gym, working on themselves instead of devoting time to children, partners, or household chores. Even as this effort to sculpt the body could simply be an acceptable form of female narcissism, it might also subvert traditional conceptions of women as devoted more to the success of others than to their own ambitions.

Figure 1. Dan Ray photograph of Gillian Kovack on stage at the 2011 IFBB North American Championships, Cleveland, Ohio, Women's Open Heavyweight Division, First Place (courtesy of Gillian Kovack).

Figure 2. Chris V. Linton photograph of Jennifer Flontek on stage at the 2011 Canadian National Bodybuilding Championships, Figure Masters Tall, Second Place (Courtesy of ChrisVLinton.com).

Figure girls strive to produce themselves as visibly toned, youthful, and well cared for, all qualities currently linked with health in dominant Western culture. At the same time, they adopt potentially dangerous behaviors to achieve this look. Some of them take anabolic steroids and inject growth hormone to increase their musculature; others undergo surgery to augment their breasts, which are diminished by diets that strip the body of fat. This extreme removal of body fat actually takes figure girls beyond the feminine ideal, revealing their well-developed shoulder caps and biceps, at odds with the softer look of Hollywood celebrities like Jennifer Aniston. Such leanness hollows out the faces of figure girls, often resulting in a taut, tired appearance equally at odds with the female visage endlessly reproduced in fashion magazines. In some ways, figure girls look and feel their worst precisely when they are being judged to see which one of them is "the best." In short, figure competitions are thoroughly paradoxical, and this aspect of them both fascinated and inspired me.

Even more appealing to me was the chance that my plan would fail, and that I would be unable to compete on stage. My literal failure was certain, for I could never win a figure competition, and would likely not even place in the top ten at an entry-level contest. Yet I longed to experience the daily grind of lifting heavy weights and the discomfort of dieting. I wished to challenge my belief system in ways that had previously been unthinkable—by wearing a bikini in front of an audience, inviting male judges to evaluate the shape of my ass, and eating meat after seventeen years as a vegetarian. Merely contemplating these acts terrified and repulsed me. I was nevertheless excited by the chance to enter, or at least to be on the edges of a bodybuilding subculture. I wanted to speak a new language about and learn a new way of seeing the human body. I was determined to push my body to its limits, studying how it responded when fueled by animal protein and supplements. Most of all, I desired to experience and demonstrate the malleability of my own body, instead of writing about the historical and cultural construction of other bodies.

As a specialist in early modern French visual culture and medicine, my previous scholarship had explored corporeality during the seventeenth century, emphasizing the representation of childbirth.[6] While implementing my new training regime and developing my methodology for the Feminist Figure Girl project, I was simultaneously writing another manuscript, *Illness as Opportunity in Early Modern France*. Based on research undertaken in archives and libraries throughout France, I gathered visual and written portrayals of convalescence to examine the shifting ways in which illness and health were defined and deployed for political ends during the seventeenth century. In Chapter Two, for example, I analyzed the celebrated anal surgery performed on Louis XIV in 1686. Although this project revealed compelling differences of the early modern body and continued to hold my interest, it did not involve the same kind of personal engagement that I attained in working on Feminist Figure Girl. All the same, I was anxious about the self-centered nature of my latest endeavor. Had I found a convenient way to legitimate the time I spent at the gym, turning my personal obsession into a research project? Was I looking for an excuse to submit to patriarchal norms by improving my appearance, reaping the unquestionable social benefits? Was I embracing a dominant culture that encouraged female self-loathing and constant efforts toward self-improvement? Or was I merely experiencing a predictable midlife crisis? Recognizing that passion and blindness are essential to productive research results, I decided to forge ahead and transform my life.

The Program

Though the sheer uncertainty of the Feminist Figure Girl project motivated me, I needed a plan. I started by telling a select few friends about my ideas, testing their reactions. They were surprised and somewhat amused but supportive. Most important to me was the opinion of Gill, my first trainer, a woman who knew my physical strengths and weaknesses and had become a confidante. To my relief, she was enthusiastic, understanding the project immediately in terms of original research rather than only the competition itself. We discussed timelines and nutrition, and she devised a targeted muscle-building program for me to follow at the gym. Only then did I reluctantly broach the topic with my partner, fearing he would be alarmed by some of the activities I was about to embrace. He expressed his legitimate concerns, but he was not at all shocked, saying, "I knew you were headed for the stage. You never do anything in half measures." I joked that he might need to move out if (or rather *when*) I became emotionally unstable as the competition neared. With typical insight, he took me seriously and began asking friends about temporary lodgings.

That weekend, while serving the Ethiopian meal I had prepared for some of my academic colleagues, I casually mentioned my new bodybuilding research project. A professor specializing in qualitative research methodologies declared that I was pursuing autoethnography, a genre I had never before encountered. She suggested several sources, agreeing to meet with me later to discuss the research protocol and ethical concerns I would need to address. I eagerly took her advice and began reading various autoethnographic studies, including works written by women who had worked as exotic dancers, survived serious illness, or struggled with eating disorders.[7] These powerful stories stressed the authors' embodied and material experience of each situation, revealing aspects of contemporary culture that could not be rationalized or analyzed using quantitative methods. For example, in her account of living as a bulimic, Lisa M. Tillmann-Healy vividly recounted the elation she felt while transporting a pint of Ben and Jerry's Cherry Garcia ice cream to her home, where she happily devoured it before efficiently vomiting into the toilet.[8]

According to social scientist Heewon Chang, autoethnography is "a research method that utilizes the researchers' autobiographical data to analyze and interpret their cultural assumptions."[9] Carolyn Ellis elaborates that "autoethnographic forms feature concrete action, emotion, embodiment, self-consciousness, and introspection portrayed in dialogue, scenes, characterization, and plot."[10] While in her own scholarship Ellis is particularly focused on the descriptive aspects of autoethnography, Jacquelyn Allen-Collinson and John Hockey emphasize self-consciousness, arguing that "autoethnographers often seek to communicate not only the immediacy, the physicality and emotionality of the experience, but also . . . the internal dialogue of the writer with her/himself."[11] These broad definitions accorded with my goals, for I wished to emphasize embodied experience, giving voice to contradiction—especially what I considered my paradoxical dual commitment to feminist politics and physical improvement—while embracing what was for me a new approach to research. When writing about early modern bodies, or the modern museums and contemporary art exhibitions that I had also examined, I had always tried to produce evocative texts highlighting a distinctive authorial voice. I had not, however, used my own life as a primary source. Rather, I had labored in archives, visited museums, interacted with art works, and produced carefully formulated theses supported by historical evidence.

I had considered autobiographical writing a nonacademic pursuit, one I engaged in only while travelling. When I was living in Paris in June 2009, for instance, I posted the following story on Facebook mainly to inform and entertain my friends.

So I Tried the French Gym

Today I decided to try the gym in my Parisian neighborhood, located beside the "Leader Price" grocery store. I reluctantly paid for a single day after being reassured that I would have access to all of the classes, including the cardio and Body Pump classes scheduled for that evening. Being early, I headed toward the weight machines. They were the overstuffed pink kind that you sometimes find in old Holiday Inns and were right beside a small, overly chlorinated swimming pool. A few men were working out, so I worked in, and though I needed to change the weights—to make them heavier!—I dared not move anything, fearing the machines would fall apart. The squat machine weight was heavy enough, however, mainly because it was so sticky with dirt and lack of care that I had a hard time getting the bar up and down.

Thankfully, the cardio class was starting, and I joined the slim French ladies in the mirrored area. This is when I entered a time warp that catapulted me back to the early 1980s, when Jane Fonda taught Jazzercise. In this case, it was a long-haired delicate Italian man leading us through what appeared to be salsa steps, with occasional knee-lifts. We were directed to spin around almost continually, not moving our arms—in a Lord of the Dance posture—and barely moving our legs. I actually started to laugh, and mouthed "C'est trop facile, monsieur." He reassured me that the class would soon get harder. He lied.

I finally left and went upstairs to use the relatively ancient rowing and elliptical machines, managing to work up a sweat while watching the zombie-like class continue below. I was feeling rather smug as I returned to the weight area, and decided to do some chest presses. I miscalculated, however, and after lowering the barbell to my chest, I could not lift it again and remained pinned like a bug until two young French men rescued me. I had forgotten that the weight numbers indicated kilograms, not pounds, and was unaware that the bar itself weighed twelve kilos. One nice young man then spotted me while I continued my work-out, and I think he even hit on me, asking me, "Vous-êtes sportive?" I was so surprised that I did not respond, for these days I am hit on only by old men with stains on their pants, not nineteen-year-old Parisians who might have a thing for sweaty middle-aged white ladies. Anyway, my superior atti-tude had been squashed, and I left the gym rather humbled, deciding I would never return.

This account is not autoethnographic for it is not particularly self-reflexive; nor does it analyze the situation in terms of social and cultural assumptions. I could potentially transform it into a more academic pursuit by considering, for example, the racial politics of the encounter—the young man who assisted me was black—or my class status, or my initial feelings of superiority with regard to the French men and women at the gym. These people were "skinny fat," a term of derision used by bodybuilders to describe those who are slender but also weak, their small frames covered in lard rather than developed musculature. It is much worse to be skinny fat than to be strong and solidly fat. Clearly, I was already thinking like a figure girl, using concepts I had learned at the gym to evaluate the bodies around me.

I did not want to engage, however, in descriptive accounts of my life that were followed by a minimal amount of explicit analy-sis, a problem with some published autoethnographies. I planned to undertake sustained observations of both myself and others, examining a range of issues, including how my material performance of gender shifted depending on my surroundings. As a person trained in visual theory and the history of the body, it made sense that I would concentrate on the visual politics of bodybuilding and draw on my historical knowledge to shape my conclusions. I envisioned a book that was simultaneously popular and scholarly, both accessible and attuned to innovative feminist theories. I wanted to make a contribution to the studies of bodybuilding, which although numerous were mostly written by outsiders who were not interested in fitness, or by ethnographers who lifted weights seriously in order to undertake participant observation, ultimately writing about the experiences of others rather than focusing on themselves.[12] Some former bodybuilders had written autobiographical accounts of their lifestyles after years of competition, shedding light on the good, the bad, and the ugly aspects of the subculture they had left.[13] To my knowledge, few if any had deliberately trained and dieted for a bodybuilding show expressly as a form of embodied research, and certainly not with the goal of analyzing the cultural, feminist, and physical aspects of figure competitions in particular. All the same, like many authors who highlight themselves in their research, I worried about being self-indulgent.[14] Perhaps my insistence on theory was meant to counteract that fear and legitimate the project, a maneuver criticized by some autoethnographic writers who defend the democratic politics of narrative against the impulse to reinscribe analytical methods.[15] Other scholars, including Chang, hold that only in-depth cultural interrogations can construct worthwhile contributions from autobiographical forays.[16]

I could hardly eschew feminist and poststructuralist theories since they had been fundamental to my development as an academic. Primarily trained in theory, I spent my years in graduate school reading Freud, Grosz, Kristeva, Derrida, Bourdieu, Gallop, and Foucault. My understandings of the "self" and "experience" continue to be informed by these and other scholars, leading me to assume that my autoethnographic pursuit would produce a fictional work that featured unstable identities, not a unique perspective or naked emotions. I approach the self as multiple and based on lack rather than plenitude, while I see experience as a limitation that determines identity—not simply in terms of the cultural and historical parameters that shape personal choices.[17] Given this framework, I was particularly drawn to the definition of autoethnography offered by Marilyn Brownstein, who contends that it "is a catastrophic encounter, a moment of vulnerability and ambiguity that is sensuous, embodied, and profoundly implicated in . . . social and ideological structures."[18] Her emphasis on a potentially destructive experience that results in the compelling confusion of new knowledge corresponded with my efforts to become Feminist Figure Girl.

Many autoethnographic studies are based on memories of illness, abuse, or personal relationships. They begin at the end, after a traumatic event has occurred and been processed.[19] In contrast, *Feminist Figure Girl* is about the practices involved in attempting to adopt another self and experience other forms of embodiment, ones that are sometimes unpleasant and sometimes fulfilling. Along with my weekly blog, this monograph was produced as the transformation occurred. While writing the better part of this introduction, for instance, I was training intensely, eating meat, taking supplements, and recording my activities in a journal. I had not yet commenced strict dieting or analyzing the interactions of bodybuilders and others at my gym according to the ethical protocols of my university. At this point, the figure competition was sixteen months away, providing a structure for, rather than a climax to, my narrative. I decided to entitle this introduction *becoming* Feminist Figure Girl because I did not and will never fully achieve that identity, which was not really my goal. Instead, I aimed to "rise to the challenge of movement" by taking physical activity seriously as a form of learning, and by considering "how culture is done in the body."[20]

I nevertheless visualized this book, bound with its table of contents, dedication page, and colorful cover photograph of me striking a figure girl pose while wearing a blue crystal-incrusted bathing suit, long before it existed. In my mind's eye, Feminist Figure Girl was a superhero, like Wonder Woman, but harder, more tanned, and better at running. According to film scholar Niall Richardson, fans of male bodybuilders identify the flexed bodies on stage with the phallus, engaging in a kind of hero worship.[21] I similarly imagined Feminist Figure Girl as a costumed heroine I would present, though my intention was not to become the phallus but to displace or re-present it imperfectly. In dialogue with the account of gender trouble produced by Judith Butler, I planned to restage myself, realizing that this heightened attention to gender identity would be primarily based on reiterated unconscious acts.[22] I wanted to undermine the notions of agency that lurk within many autoethnographic studies, and was curious about whether these actions would produce a standard stereotype with little political and social impact, or something much more interesting. In the end, I learned much from my experiment, which, as I argue in the following chapters, had multiple and unexpected results, ultimately challenging and changing my understandings of feminism, the body, and the potential for acts of stillness as well as movement to produce radical transformation.

Chapter Outlines

Chapter One: Measuring Up: Comparing Bodybuilding, Weight Watchers, and Yoga

Based on six months of naturalistic observation undertaken at my gym, at local Weight Watchers meetings, and during hatha yoga classes, this chapter lays the groundwork for the more theoretical discussions of bodybuilding developed in subsequent chapters by comparing the kinds of bodies produced in all three practices, examining them in terms of visuality, epistemology, and notions of sustenance. Visuality moves beyond biological understandings of seeing to examine historically and culturally specific ways of looking at the world.[23] Chapter One analyzes both the explicit and implicit kinds of visual training I received while preparing for the figure competition, during my instruction in the Weight Watchers program, and from my yoga teachers. I consider how my body was transformed into a visual object subject to a specific kind of scrutiny at the gym, one that focused on the articulation of individual muscles rather than the numerical assessment encouraged by the Weight Watchers program.[24] These transformed bodies furthermore contrasted sharply with the emphasis on inner vision and release of the ego promoted by yoga. My continued comparisons of the three practices, which address their conceptions of bodily knowledge, and the relationships they forge between bodies and food or energy, nevertheless reveal significant areas of overlap between them. The final results might be surprising, for I contend that while Weight Watchers is thoroughly disciplinary in a Foucauldian sense, bodybuilding is closer to yoga than to the corporate diet program, similarly embracing the body itself as a site for knowledge production, and ultimately accepting its weaknesses.

Chapter Two: Embodiment and the Event of Muscle Failure

Chapter Two explores the specific bodily sensations experienced during weight lifting, drawing on Maurice Merleau-Ponty's arguments about flesh and embodiment to explore muscle failure.[25] Failure is deliberately achieved when tired muscles can no longer perform a repetition and obstinately refuse to budge, foregrounding the sheer materiality of the body. This chapter engages with Merleau-Ponty's theories alongside the models of feminist phenomenology developed by Simone de Beauvoir and Iris Marion Young, considering the gendered embodied subjectivity of figure girl training, while differentiating figure competitions from heavyweight, fitness, and bikini contests.[26] I highlight the recalcitrant materiality of the female body as it refuses to be productive, rather than focusing exclusively on longstanding efforts to manage that body. Whereas much previous scholarship on bodybuilding has framed it in terms of mastery and the pursuit of both discipline and pain, I argue that muscle failure promotes a kind of physical experience reducible neither to pain nor to the transcendence of the flesh.[27] I contend that weight lifting introduces the body to a range of novel sensations, sometimes mistaken for pain because they do not fall easily within the domain of comfort, often promoted as the only desirable kind of sensation within our contemporary consumer culture. The limits of the flesh and a wider array of physicality are fundamental to bodybuilding training, potentially reconfiguring what Merleau-Ponty calls the body schema, and creating a kind of exhilaration in keeping with Foucault's advocacy of countering power with "the claims of bodies, pleasures, and knowledges, in their multiplicity and their possibility of resistance."[28]

Chapter Three: Replacing Feminism: Comparing Prochoice Activism with Becoming a Figure Girl

Figure girls apparently strive to be considered sexually attractive, posing in tiny bikinis while wearing stiletto heels. They transform their bodies in order to attract the gaze, inviting audiences to look at and admire their physical achievements. This potentially heightened sex appeal might seem at odds with feminist goals, and certainly other than such prochoice acts as political lobbying and clinic escorting, in which I have also engaged. This chapter will compare and contrast my work in the reproductive rights movement with my transformation into a figure competitor. In keeping with my interest in embodied experience, I ask, What does it feel like to be a bodybuilder? Is it utterly distinct from being a prochoice activist? Is it possible to embody feminism? And, if so, what would that feel like? After comparing prochoice activism and bodybuilding in terms of physicality and the creation of embodied communality among women, I conclude by finding more similarities among, than differences between, the two performative practices.

Chapter Four: On Stage: Performing Feminist Figure Girl

Chapter Four is in many ways the narrative climax of this book, providing an examination of the impact of finally staging Feminist Figure Girl during my competition in June 2011. In order to consider the performative aspects of this display, and the scripted poses that it required, I compare my project with the contemporary work of both the performance artist Marina Abramović and the visual artist Heather Cassils. Abramović's longstanding valorization of corporeal stillness, and the deliberate pursuit of it as a kind of bodily discipline, led me to analyze my (futile) attempts to strike and hold figure girl postures on stage as an important form of labor, made legible within the broader economic demands and desires for physical constraint within contemporary capitalist culture. Cassils likewise attends to the materiality of the lived body in a number of provocative works, understanding it as produced within particular economic and historical conditions, but goes further than Abramović by rendering palpable the labor of "doing gender." Cassils's representations of trans identity challenged me to address my own efforts to reproduce gender while staging Feminist Figure Girl, acknowledging my enabling position as a white heterosexual and mostly female-identified professor.

Chapter Five: Aftermath: The Photographs in My Purse

After the Mr. Olympia competition featured in *Pumping Iron* (1977), the male bodybuilders, including Arnold Schwarzenegger and Lou Ferrigno, dash backstage to smoke a joint while eating fried chicken and cake. Chapter Five presents my own experiences of what happened after the figure contest of 2011, extending far beyond the immediate euphoria of postshow carb-loading. The chapter's title refers to the photographs taken the day of the competition and subsequently offered up to the media as evidence of my achievement.

Like many figure girls and bodybuilders, I carried smaller versions of these images in my purse for months afterward, eagerly displaying them to anyone who wanted to look. In this final chapter, I analyze the status and multiple functions of photography in relation to the practice of bodybuilding, focusing on images of me training, posing for my weekly progress pictures, and exhibiting myself on stage. I am primarily interested in the continual alteration and mobility of what at first glance appears to be still images. Drawing on recent photographic theory, I approach these images as performative sites that do work rather than simply describe or represent events. I contend that photographic technologies are a crucial part of the collaborative production, rather than the mere representation, of bodybuilding/figure identities. I then examine a series of photographs taken by artist Patrick J. Reed as I was training, cooking, and preparing for my competition. These images highlight the labor of constructing my body, revealing its dependence on a community of supporters. I pay particular attention to the group shots in which I appear to be weak and vulnerable, offering them as feminist alternatives to the standard pictures of isolated figure girls standing on stage, looking glamorous and triumphant.

1

Measuring Up

Comparing Bodybuilding,
Weight Watchers, and Yoga

I enter a dank room in the basement of the old gymnasium building, noticing that it smells of chlorine. Clutching a plastic bag containing a black bathing suit and towel, I am ready to have my BMI (body mass index) measured accurately at the Sport and Health Assessment Centre on the university campus where I work. In the corner, a metal chair attached to a pulley mechanism hovers above a strangely narrow and deep swimming pool. A technician explains the procedure: I must sit in the chair and blow out my breath—every last bit of it—before she lowers me to the bottom of the pool, calculates the amount of water displaced, and then pulls me back out. I begin to have doubts as I awkwardly climb into the chair. My sense of alarm increases when the young woman places a heavy weight belt across my lap to ensure that I remain submerged, like one of Dexter's body bags. I wonder if I should mention that I suffer from claustrophobia, but decide against it. During the first two attempts, I panic as soon as the water covers my nose, and the technician immediately yanks me out. I am terrified and shaking. The third time I rest briefly on the bottom before I freak out, waving my arms while trying to dislodge the chunky belt. This is getting embarrassing. Steeling myself, I finally manage to remain underwater and slowly count to ten. When I emerge, the technician reports that her readings are too high and decides I must be taking a small breath of air before going under. She is correct. Apparently, my body's uncontrollable will to live is thwarting the pursuit of science. Another lab worker then enters the room to suggest that I continue to take a shallow breath and then expel it into a measuring instrument—it looks like a breathalyzer—as soon as I break the surface. I am plunged into the water three more times, and finally the announcement is made: I have 16.2 percent body fat, which in addition to the results of my strength testing, puts me in the 95th percentile for women my age. I am ecstatic . . . until I remember that I probably must achieve an eight percent fat level for my figure competition in June 2011, just over nine months away.

When I describe this harrowing experience to my partner later that day, he compares it to the gruesome execution scene at the beginning of Michel Foucault's *Discipline and Punish*, first published in English in 1977.[1] I laughingly protest, noting that my limbs are still attached to my body. I nevertheless realize that he has a point. The water torture I endured was a kind of disciplinary mechanism that transformed my body into knowledge, rendering it numerically legible. This normalizing process informed me that I have a lower amount of fat and higher amount of musculature than most women aged thirty-five to forty-five, rewarding me for conforming to the current ideal of the lean female body. Since my "above average" physical condition was produced by systematically lifting weights and consuming protein, I begin to wonder if bodybuilding is best understood as a disciplinary practice, creating docile subjects easily controlled by liberal forms of governmentality.[2] This Foucauldian interpretation of both bodybuilding and the contemporary fitness culture would hardly be novel. It is promoted in a range of scholarship, including that of Brian Pronger, who argues that sculpting the body through weight training can be considered a fascist act undermining opportunities for physical transcendence.[3]

At first glance, this claim seems applicable to my own regime. For the past eighteen months I have been lifting weights for about two hours almost every day, performing five sets of five different exercises for each body part: back, biceps, triceps, chest, shoulders, and legs. I have taken precisely timed rests of sixty seconds between each set or superset, and have ended my sessions with a cardio workout consisting of either a rousing spin class or an uphill march on the treadmill. I have also regularly changed aspects of this routine to "shock my body," lest it become complacent and refuse to grow.

At the gym I have recorded my progress in a small booklet, while continually surveying myself in the mirror both to monitor my technique and to look for signs of improvement. My goal has been to achieve a visibly muscular X shape, with wide shoulders and lats that taper into a narrow waist and then flare out again with chiseled glutes and hams.

All the same, I reject the idea that bodybuilding can be fully understood in terms of discipline and self-surveillance. Maybe I am embracing conformity or else proving Foucault's point that "where there is power, there is resistance," albeit always from within regimes of power.[4] All the same, accounts of self-mastery do not accord with my diverse experiences of lifting weights and working out, which have included exhaustion and a sense of triumph but have also induced muscle failure and sudden endorphin rushes. I decide to investigate further, inventing a research plan that ultimately results in this chapter. In the discussion below, I distinguish bodybuilding from other physical regimes that I have also used to transform my body, namely the Weight Watchers diet program and hatha yoga. My comparison is based on six months of naturalistic observation, unobtrusively undertaken from September 2010 through February 2011, while I worked out at the gym, regularly weighed in at Weight Watchers meetings, and enrolled in beginner hatha yoga classes.[5] During this time I was attentive to how each activity approached, represented, and promoted the creation of particular kinds of bodies, though I should note that in keeping with my autoethnographic methodology I focused on my privileged, white, Canadian, straight, female, then forty-three-year-old body.[6]

As I performed my observations, I narrowed in on three main themes: visuality, epistemology, and sustenance. For the first theme I analyzed how each practice positioned the body in relation to vision, considering whether or not my body was produced as an object to be looked at or displayed, and how both I and other participants were taught to regard bodies in general. In terms of the second theme, epistemology, I investigated how the three activities portrayed bodies as sites for the creation of knowledge, addressing the roles of such authority figures as personal trainers, meeting leaders, and yoga teachers in this knowledge production. The third theme, sustenance, invoked nourishment and food, crucial topics for both bodybuilders and followers of Weight Watchers, but also could embrace the more spiritual kind of sustenance central to the practice of yoga. In this case, I was concerned with how each practice understood the body in relation to concepts of energy.

Some of the findings I outline below will likely be unsurprising to readers. I insist, for example, that the Weight Watchers program is the most disciplinary practice in a Foucauldian sense, transforming my body into a manageable object in accordance with dominant values, and yoga the least so. Other conclusions might be less expected, for in the end I argue that bodybuilding had more in common with my yoga classes than the Weight Watchers regime. I found that bodybuilding was not entirely normalizing; it was in many ways an open and flexible practice. My sustained comparison indicated that bodybuilding could embrace unique bodies, exploring and even accepting their physical weaknesses. This conclusion is at odds with much previous scholarship that links bodybuilding with physical mastery and the pursuit of masculine dominance, or in the case of female bodybuilders, with either the acceptance or refusal of repressive forms of femininity.[7] Thus in this chapter I move toward an alternative interpretation of the appeal of bodybuilding, even as I am careful to avoid minimizing its disciplinary effects.

Looking at Bodies

According to the March 2010 edition of *Women's Health Magazine*, 18 percent of women check themselves out in the mirror ten or more times a day.[8] I find this statistic surprisingly low. Since I have begun bodybuilding in a serious way, I constantly gaze at my reflection, far surpassing that average. Every wall and support beam in my downtown gym is encased in mirrors, creating multiple images of patrons as they use the weight machines, replace dumbbells, or simply walk to the water fountain. The gym is a site of spectacle, arguably even more than it is a location for exercise. Yet there is a particularly intense kind of looking that bodybuilders learn. I was taught by my first personal trainer, a competitive heavyweight bodybuilder, to regard isolated muscles, ensuring both that they were working through the full range of motion and that my technique was proper, rather than liable to cause injury. This kind of seeing has now become second nature to me, like periodically glancing in the rearview mirror while driving. When seated in the leg-extension machine, for example, I look in the mirror during every other repetition to confirm that my quads are noticeably flexing and that my straight back is resting against the chair, contributing little to the movement. When working out, I am attuned to the mechanics of particular parts of my body, not to my overall physique or appearance.

I regularly consider my body from head to toe, but not while in the gym proper. I pose secretly, behind closed doors in a small room with my new personal trainer, an amateur boxer. Every six weeks since I began working with her, I quickly change into my vintage 1950s pink bikini encrusted with rhinestones and stand against a blank wall while she uses my cheap digital camera to take four full-length photos of me as I make quarter-turns, discussed more in Chapter Five. We scrutinize these pictures, comparing them with the previous set, discussing any physical changes or improvements. We are looking specifically for increased mass in my lats and glutes, and more definition throughout my back. These pictures prove that I am growing my back and that my ass is "perking up," to use the phrase employed by my young trainer. Such changes are difficult to see when I look at myself in the mirror, or gaze down at my body. In that sense, my (semi) built body exists only in photographs; it is other than me; it is objectified.

This objectification carries into the working areas of the gym, where I increasingly attract the approving gazes of both men and women, especially those who train regularly and can note my progress. Sometimes this looking is positive, and I welcome it. For instance, I once heard two male bodybuilders remark "she is strong" while watching me do multiple sets of deep walking lunges with a ninety-pound barbell on my shoulders. At other times, this looking sexualizes me. I do not like it when creepy men in jogging pants make kissing sounds as I pass by them on my way to the spin studio (though this rarely happens), but I enjoy it when hot potentially lesbian or bi women and straight or bi men give me the once over. I now take pride in my body and newly upright posture, something I have never done in the past. I also relish my newfound "body awareness" as I feel my engaged or sore muscles almost continually, having a sense of my physique both in motion and at rest. This awareness has influenced other parts of my life, for better or worse. I now spend time applying makeup, arranging my long, dyed-blonde hair, and paying for regular microdermabrasion sessions. I also notice the fatty deposits worsening my already pronounced eye bags, and wonder what to do about them.

Paying attention to every aspect of my bodily appearance is appropriate for an aspiring figure girl. Figure competitions involve creating not only the muscled and dieted body shape noted above, but include what advice books and online preparation guides refer to as "the whole package."[9] Presenting this package involves caring for skin, hair, and nails because figure girls are judged not only on the size, proportion, and ideal visibility of their muscles but are required to have healthy locks, a glowing complexion, and impressive poise as they strike the mandatory quarter-turn poses and walk while wearing regulation stiletto heels. These girls do not talk, giving their opinions about world hunger and childcare as do Miss America contestants.[10] Nor do they adopt such standard muscular poses as "front double biceps" like the light-, middle-, and heavyweight bodybuilders of both sexes. You will not see figure girls do one-arm pushups or back flips on stage—though some of them probably could—in keeping with the routines performed by female fitness competitors. Figure girls simply display their bodies from all sides in a manner that resembles a beauty pageant as much as a bodybuilding contest.

One explanation for the relatively recent invention of figure competitions—the first National Physique Committee (NPC) Figure Nationals was held in 2001, and the first official contest sponsored by the International Federation of Bodybuilding (IFBB) was in 2003—is that they deliberately counteract the supposed masculinization of female heavyweight bodybuilding.[11] The larger and stronger those impressive women get, the more alternative competitions insist on conventional forms of feminine appearance and behavior. Yet even figure girls might be considered too muscular and thus potentially threatening to the gendered status quo, prompting the introduction of bikini competitions in which thin, large-breasted women skip across the stage and pose provocatively in distinction from the relatively wooden presentations of figure girls. While watching the first bikini contest at the 2010 Olympia in Las Vegas—the most prestigious event in bodybuilding, which includes the crowning of Mr. and Ms. Olympia as well as the Figure Olympia—I overheard serious bodybuilders assert that bikini girls were not athletes who worked out and deserved recognition; they were just tanned young women with breast implants and glittery swimsuits, performing for a lucrative heterosexual male demographic.

The participants in both figure and bikini competitions are diverse, ranging in age, social class, background, and ethnicity, though these groups have not yet been studied by scholars employing either quantitative or ethnographic methods.[12] Online searches related to figure competitions in particular reveal that they are regularly held throughout North America, as well as in the Philippines, South America, Australia, Europe, the United Kingdom, South Africa, and Korea, typically sponsored by local organizations. My show, for example, was managed by the Alberta Bodybuilding Association (www.abba.ab.ca), in affiliation with the larger Canadian Bodybuilding Federation (cbbf.ca) and International Federation of Bodybuilding and Fitness (www.ifbb.com), which helped to shape the contest's regulations. Though such recognized groups finance annual or biannual competitions with membership dues, entry fees, and ticket sales, most figure girls expend personal funds to pay for their training, posing suits, tanning regimes, and diet coaches. A few competitors attract some corporate sponsorship, but many aspiring figure girls accumulate debt in order to participate in shows. All the same, the competitions attract consistent interest, with over 50 figure girls and well over 100 bikini girls entering even the relatively small, local contests. These statements are, however, necessarily based on my personal experiences, as the demographic makeup and differing ambitions of figure girls remain largely unknown. I can report only that none of the aspiring figure girls who I met had relished the "beauty contest" aspects of the shows; they were instead committed to developing muscle mass before decreasing levels of body fat. More interested in the process than the result, they viewed the onstage display of their bodies as a challenging goal offering ultimate proof of their months and years of willpower and dedication, rather than a temporary revelation of beauty or poise. There is certainly a competitive aspect to the visible display of muscular development, the sole physical trait shared by all serious figure contestants. A standard view among figure girls, for example, is that those women who are new to the practice, or who cheat on their diets, are demoted to the level of bikini girls, the "lowest rung" of competition. All the same, it remains difficult for me to generalize about figure contestants, as during my own training I might simply have encountered a number of particularly athletic and ambitious figure girls within specific settings—primarily at Canadian gyms and events—who engaged with me because they could identify with my embodied research project.

One thing I can say is that my experiences both at the gym and watching various kinds of competitions have taught me how to see bodies—those of others and my own—in terms of muscularity, leanness, and proportion. Various pedagogical experiences, including direct instructions from professionals, posing at the gym and at official posing workshops, consulting online resources, and attending local and international competitions, have immersed me in a particular form of visuality, a term increasingly used by art historians and other scholars. The study of visuality moves beyond biological understandings of seeing to examine historically and culturally specific ways of looking at the world. For the past twenty years or so, specialists of visual culture have explored the shifting nature of vision, ranging from medieval China to nineteenth-century optometry, to consider how looking has changed over time.[13] Art historian Hal Foster encourages the investigation of modern culture in terms of "how we see, how we are able, allowed or made to see, and how we see this seeing or the unseen therein."[14] This approach reveals how looking not only changes over time and across cultures but also within them. Anthropologist Sarah Franklin, for example, recounts how she was unable to discern the nuclei of stem cells beneath an electron microscope until given extended lessons by embryologist Sue Pickering.[15] In my role as a university professor, I regularly instruct art history students to regard visual culture by undertaking formal analyses of composition, line, and color, primarily interpreting images in relation to other images. This method of looking often takes years to develop. Bodybuilding also produces a particular way of looking that is painstakingly learned but eventually seems natural and can be applied to any body. It is now difficult for me not to see the world through the lens of muscular leanness and development. In fact, I entitled one feministfiguregirl.com blog entry "When Did I Become Such an Asshole?" because I found myself judging the skinny and obese bodies around me and feeling disdain for their weakness.

There is little overlap between the visuality produced in bodybuilding culture and that promoted by the Weight Watchers diet program. Though I noted some distinctive features at the Weight Watchers meetings I attended in Canada, the United States, France, and England (more about that below), they all had at least one thing in common: a notable lack of mirrors. Visible self-appraisal is not a prominent part of the Weight Watchers doctrine, which is almost entirely focused on numbers. When members first register for the program, they are immediately weighed, and that number is written down in their official tracker. Each week, they bring the small pamphlet with them, step onto the scale, and see whether or not their number has changed. If it has decreased, they will receive praise and possibly a sticker, especially if they have lost a five- or ten-pound increment. If the number has increased, they will be encouraged to continue with the program, reassured that consistency will eventually produce results. Any bodily display at Weight Watchers meetings is inadvertent, produced when members strip off their heavy clothes and shoes to achieve the lowest possible number on the scale. Looking good is equated with weighing less and getting smaller; it has nothing to do with visible musculature, physical strength, groomed hair, or well-applied makeup.

The Weight Watchers program ostensibly improves self-esteem, with members gaining social approval through their weight loss. They generally strive to "fit in" and feel more comfortable in such social situations as high school reunions, weddings, and holiday parties. In contrast, figure girls work to craft an exceptional body that will stand out in every location, especially at the gym. After some visual training, it is easy to recognize the distinctively sculpted look of the figure girl, but there is no way to identify a fellow Weight Watcher outside of a meeting context, unless she brandishes a 10 percent goal award on her key chain, or has corporate food items in her grocery cart. There is no ideal body shape in Weight Watchers; any body that gets smaller and falls within the "healthy weight range" for its height is considered a success. As someone who is five feet four inches, for instance, I can choose a goal weight anywhere between 117 and 146 pounds; a body weight under or over this range is deemed both unhealthy and undesirable.

I first joined Weight Watchers in 2005, when I lived in another Canadian city. I signed up for the obligatory initial five weeks to gather information about the regime and to try its principles. Then I simply weighed in each week at my gym, with other women who were following the program in a strict fashion. After about six months, I had lost thirty pounds and, in contrast to the experiences of most dieters, I have never regained them, likely because of my consistently intense workouts and altered eating habits. A few years later, I moved to the city in which I currently live and decided to lose another ten pounds. I rejoined Weight Watchers, explaining to the leader that my standards were now higher and selecting 125 pounds as my goal. This time, however, I attended the weekly meetings, getting to know the leader and enjoying the camaraderie of the regulars. Within a few months, I had reached my goal weight and received my lifetime membership card along with a silver star for my key chain. My body was on display when I was called to the front of the room to tell the story of my "journey" in true self-help fashion. Since I had begun bodybuilding in earnest, I happily showed off my "guns" by wearing a skimpy tank top to this awards ceremony. In order to retain my lifetime status, I was obliged to weigh in once each month, avoiding the $16.20 meeting fee as long as I remained within two pounds of my goal weight.

Yet bodybuilding ultimately undermined my success at Weight Watchers, highlighting the conflict between the two practices. Shortly after achieving lifetime status, I began to increase my muscle mass. As I became less fat, I started to weigh more. My weight steadily increased from 125 to 140, and each month I paid the meeting fee as a punishment for my "failure." On one hand, I found the situation amusing because I was far fitter and leaner than everyone else at the meetings I was attending, including the leaders. On the other hand, I was annoyed by the lack of recognition of my achievement, and by the rigid insistence on maintaining a static skinny-fat body instead of pursuing a muscular physique. My situation did not go unnoticed, however, and it even disrupted the corporate policies of Weight Watchers. I paste here an excerpt from my journal, written after I received an e-mail from the primary leader at my meetings:

> I received an e-mail from the leader at WW who usually weighs me in at meetings. She had googled me and found my public e-mail listed at the university but was still tentative about contacting me because of the strict privacy policy at WW. She had seen me weigh in over my goal weight of 125 (today I was 134) and have to pay the meeting fee.

She asked to meet me for coffee, saying that she felt it was wrong that as I got stronger and built muscle I nevertheless had to pay the fee. She wanted to gain muscle and asked me for advice. I met her and liked her a lot. I found this exchange fascinating because I am in effect defying the WW ideology and am causing some problems for one of the leaders. I recommended that she eat more protein, find a good trainer, and lift really heavy weights, with fewer reps like I do. She said that as she gets older—she is now mid 50s—counting points alone is not working. Even as she eats fewer points she gains weight. She also bought a scale that measures BMI and was shocked that it measured her at 36% fat, which is quite high. . . . I weighed in with this leader this morning and she wrote down my increased weight but did not calculate the number of pounds that I was up. I see this as a form of resistance on her part.

In her examination of Weight Watchers meetings, feminist philosopher Cressida Heyes draws on Foucauldian theory to argue that they simultaneously produce an atmosphere of female solidarity and enforce mechanisms of self-surveillance meant to normalize behavior.[16] Heyes is correct, and I discuss the solidarity of the meetings below, but my personal experiences revealed more wiggle room in terms of self-surveillance, indicating that even some leaders could doubt and challenge the official corporate program. I subsequently learned that the leader who contacted me began training with a former figure girl, lifting heavy weights, and eating increased amounts of protein, following a diet that was in no way based on the Weight Watchers points system. In this instance, my muscular body disrupted and contradicted the Weight Watchers ideal, suggesting that the disciplined eating and measuring of the diet program were distinct from the practices associated with bodybuilding.

In terms of visuality, yoga similarly has little in common with bodybuilding; nor does it accord with Weight Watchers. Yogic practice does not involve scrutinizing the muscles of the body, or looking intently at numbers on a scale. Just this morning, my yoga instructor insisted that we should avoid the distraction of vision, arguing that seeing interferes with our concentration. I was initially surprised when almost every hatha yoga class that I took in a mirrorless studio a few blocks from my condo similarly began with the leader asking us to close our eyes and attend to breathing. We often remained with eyes closed for many minutes and were continually reminded to avoid looking at others, focusing only on ourselves. "This is not a competition," the teacher would say in a low, soothing voice. "Do not force your movements. Send your breath into any stiff or sore body part as you practice the poses. Just see where your body is today, and what it wants to do, which might not be the same as last time. That's fine." Any looking we did was interior, in the mind's eye, without picturing the body as an object of scrutiny or control. Instead, this interior vision encouraged us to become mindful embodied subjects, experiencing movement and stillness while grounded to the earth and infused with life-giving breath.

My personal trainer had advised me to enroll in yoga classes as a kind of antidote to bodybuilding. Whereas weight lifting shortened, tightened, and bulked the muscles, yoga would stretch, lengthen, and relax them, ultimately rewarding me with a more pleasing physique on stage. This understanding of yoga as a healthy stretch rather than a religious or spiritual endeavor is now commonplace in Western culture, encouraged by the increasing commodification of the practice since the 1960s.[17] As yoga has become more popular, a wider range of adaptations have become available, including hot yoga and power yoga, forms that might scarcely be recognized as yoga by those with more traditional or "authentic" training. A number of scholarly studies have recently explored the expansion of yoga in the West, commenting on the concurrent appropriation and erasure of its spiritual and political elements, as well as on the commercialization of yoga as just another fitness option.[18] Name brand yoga mats and clothing are among the most obvious signs of this contemporary culture, but participants can also strive to attain a "yoga body." This long, flexible, and supple body has itself become a kind of cultural capital, distinguished from lumpier or more rigid ones, especially when clad in Lululemon attire. In this sense, there is a visuality to yoga, or at least a yogic style, but this kind of looking was not part of my hatha classes, taken on my days off from training at the gym. Potentially more spiritual than power yoga, my hatha classes emphasized breathing, meditation, relaxation, and chanting, along with the technical mastery of such poses as the downward dog. Although I was initially convinced that bodybuilding and yoga were entirely different kinds of activities, additional physical and intellectual engagement with each allowed me to perceive areas of overlap.

Knowing the Body

There are a number of ways to learn about the built body, including online resources, professional trainers, YouTube videos, and such books as *Women's Strength Training Anatomy*, currently resting on the shelf beside me.[19] Yet in the end, reading and listening are not adequate methods of comprehending the practice of bodybuilding: it must be physically experienced, for the body itself is the primary locus of knowledge. The importance of participation and corporeal movement is embedded in the language of bodybuilding; weight lifters train their muscles, which acquire muscle memory in order to perform repetitions properly. This interaction with muscles is not unidirectional, however, and it is common to hear someone at the gym explain that their biceps or glutes are "talking to them," making their presence known after an intense workout the day before. People new to bodybuilding will endure novel sensations as they strengthen their tendons slowly in order to lift heavier weights and grow larger muscles. After targeting individual muscles and muscle groups with increased weights, they will come to appreciate delayed onset muscle soreness (DOMS) as they rest to allow for repair while eating hundreds of grams of protein.

Even as I follow the standard regime of working out, resting, and eating, I am at this point in 2011 a bodybuilding neophyte, having trained seriously with weights for a mere three years, and consumed adequate protein for only one, relinquishing a seventeen-year-long vegetarian diet to pursue the allure of beefiness. Credibility as a bodybuilder requires a far more extensive period of muscle manipulation, often leading to participation in contests. According to my observations, bodybuilders are truly respected as athletes once they compete, and will likely not be acknowledged within the subculture until they have competed many times. This necessity is part of paying one's dues and demonstrating persistence but relates as well to the importance of extensive bodily experimentation. The results gained through trial and error with different kinds of workouts, food consumption, supplementation, dieting, and fat-loading must be displayed on stage and judged by a panel of experts, themselves former competitors.

I recently purchased *Figure Competition Secrets*, a book written by figure girl Karen Sessions. She starts with a disclaimer: "the author of the provided material is not a licensed physician. The knowledge acquired has been obtained through years of extensive research and personal experimentation."[20] It soon becomes clear that for Sessions research and corporeal experimentation are the same thing. She describes how over the years she has evaluated different supplements, diuretics, training programs, diets, and tanning creams by testing them on her own body and observing the results. Sessions's body is essentially a science project, and she insists that:

> I developed a keen interest in how the body works in relation to food and exercise. With that, I took my training to the next level and began entering bodybuilding contests. The constant challenges kept me on edge to keep building and reshaping my physique. This makes me uniquely qualified to help you meet your fitness goals.[21]

Her book explains what worked for her and urges serious figure girls to try the suggestions for themselves, making adjustments according to the unique requirements of their own personal flesh.

This emphasis on first-hand lived experience and empirical wisdom reminds me of the early modern period, when bodily knowledge was respected. Women could speak authoritatively about childbirth, for example, after having been pregnant and in labor many times.[22] Those who had given birth to only a few children would be laughed out of the lying-in chamber; women who had never visibly demonstrated their fertility might be excluded altogether from the pushing, panting, wine drinking, and female-only conversation linked with reproduction during that era. One hopes those unfortunate souls would have at least had a phantom pregnancy or some kind of menstrual irregularities to compensate for their lack of bodily knowledge. Or maybe they could theatrically produce a few rabbits from their not-so-barren-after-all wombs, like the infamous Mary Toft, a prolific woman in eighteenth-century England who fooled more than a few physicians.[23]

In figure and other kinds of bodybuilding contests, the body is likewise a crucial source of knowledge; it is scrutinized, tested, and to a certain degree managed. Yet the built body remains unpredictable and in flux, not perfected or conquered. Though there is a standard regime, each body is unique, and bodybuilders must pay careful attention to their particular physiques in order to succeed. They must see whether or not certain muscles grow faster than others—for instance, I have proportionately large traps, so I avoid doing weighted shoulder shrugs—and how their bodies react to carbohydrates, cardio training, and particular brands of fat burners. Even as the built body is considered a machine, becoming compartmentalized and objectified, it emerges as an individualized entity, with specific strengths and weaknesses. I have a naturally small waist and strong core, so my training is focused on my flabby glutes and relatively unimpressive back. Other shortcomings are related to my work as a professor who writes books and articles, resulting in serious tendonitis in both wrists. I also have boney fusion in both feet, a birth defect that regularly impedes my ability to do such cardio training as stair running and sprints, as does the longstanding Achilles injury in my left ankle. Instead of forcing my body into an ideal shape, I have learned to listen to it, both cursing and accepting its limitations. In the end, this kind of engagement in bodybuilding is commonplace because the goal is to discover what the body can do and how far it will go and responding to what you learn.

In this sense, bodybuilding overlaps with the practice of yoga, in which the body is not an object to be mastered but an essence deserving of respect. In yoga, every body is different, and these differences must be discovered, cherished, and challenged. Learning about yoga similarly requires embodied engagement and consistent practice, but such practice does not always take the form of physical movement. It can also involve philosophical reflection, listening, or meditation, both alone and in a group. According to yoga guru Kate Potter, host of the popular television program *Namaste Yoga*:

> Yoga in the West has become overidentified with the physical, with the form, and with the fashion of the form. This is problematic. . . . The idea of yoga is to take care of our physical limitations and get beyond our self-obsession. We

learn that we can let go of this ego identification and have a
glimpse of a much wider field of experience. If one is looking for progress, or results, then one is already off the path
according to yoga. Even when we refer just to the physical
practice, striving is not the route.[24]

Potter indicates that taking care of physical limitations is key to
yoga, an element in common with bodybuilding, but also notes that
progress per se is not the point, for unlike the practice of weight lifting, yoga is not goal oriented.

Nor is yoga competitive. Comparing one's yoga practice to that
of another is egotistical, whereas many forms of yoga—and there
are so many different kinds that this generalizing discussion can in
no way do justice to any of them—are about dissolving the ego and
working to unify the mind, spirit, and body. Yoga emphasizes genu-
ine effort more than results. When I dropped into a vinyasa yoga
class at my gym the other day, I took note when the instructor ended
by asking us to appreciate the opportunity we had had to practice
together, and to acknowledge the effort that everyone had made.
Although consistent effort is certainly admired in bodybuilding, that
practice is driven by the goal of achieving larger, stronger muscles, or
an improved appearance on stage. Bodybuilding contests involve the
comparison of bodies, most obviously when competitors are called
out in pairs and asked to do the same pose side by side, and during
the theatrical pose down at the end of judging, when bodybuilders jockey for both space on the stage and the visual attention of an
audience. Yoga practitioners are never subjected to this kind of judgment, given a prize, or ranked in order of ability.

All the same, like seasoned bodybuilders, yoga practitioners can
become distinguished experts. Their authority may be based on a
variety of factors and can change according to context, but it helps
if they have had a longstanding commitment to yoga practice and
meditation, have participated in yoga retreats, or been trained in
an important ashram, especially one in India.[25] According to my
rather limited observations, yoga instructors typically exhibit a certain demeanor, emanating an aura of peace and tranquility, and a
generosity of spirit that involves listening to others and desiring to
help them. Perhaps yoga authorities can be said to possess a kind
of spiritual capital, in keeping with Bourdieu's notion of cultural

capital, although capital in relation to yoga might be offensive to some adherents.[26] Yoga authorities also display signs of self-care, as according to Cressida Heyes, "yoga is a somatic practice that is not about discipline or pain (though there are rules and it can be very hard work)."[27] There is no congruent disposition for a competitive bodybuilder, though of course generosity and kindness are always welcomed. To outsiders, the bodybuilding identity is visual rather than spiritual, revealed by cut musculature, tanned skin, and an upright posture. To insiders, it is a particular form of embodied labor and fleshly know-how, made visibly evident.

The Weight Watchers regime could not be more different from that of both bodybuilding and yoga. Adherents to the diet program learn about the body from designated leaders who explain what they call a "scientifically based approach to weight loss," and hand out written instructions.[28] Clients are positioned as recipients of the research done by experts, and this information grounds a system that must be followed, with little room for experimentation. When members first join they must quickly select a goal weight, determined by measuring their current weight, height, and BMI, which can be done online at the official website (weightwatchers. com). When I recently entered my data into this program, it calculated my BMI at 24. This number is clearly too high, revealing the way in which all bodies are reduced to numerical entities within the normalizing operations of the Weight Watchers program, without regard for muscular development or such factors as age, class status, ethnicity, "race," or disability.

The corporate program can produce a sense of disembodiment as those bodies reduced to numbers are treated similarly. The Weight Watchers regime assumes that every human body will respond to a calorie-reduced diet by shedding fat. The amount of calories consumed is established by a points system in which all food items are allotted a numerical value. These points have been designated by scientific experts and are both posted on the Weight Watchers website and available in printed booklets, but members can also use their "points calculator," a kind of slide rule that combines number of calories, grams of fiber, and grams of fat per serving to produce a number. A fifty-calorie serving of nonfat yogurt, for example, would be one point. The number of points eaten by each adherent to the Weight Watchers system is based on his or her weight and height.

When I rejoined the program, I was allowed to eat twenty points worth of food per day, and was encouraged to measure and keep track of every single thing that I consumed.

The Weight Watchers mantra nevertheless touts its flexibility, a claim based on the fact that followers can choose which foods to eat instead of purchasing the prepared meals promoted by other weight-loss programs.[29] For lunch, a Weight Watchers adherent can decide to have a serving of low-fat cottage cheese and a lightly dressed salad topped with walnuts for six points, or a small, high-fat bar of chocolate for the same number of points. In both cases she is obeying the program and should lose weight. Though eating healthy food is encouraged, it is by no means obligatory. Another example of consumer choice is the thirty-five "flex" points that can be added to the weekly food allotment, either all at once (in what bodybuilders would call a cheat meal) or dispersed throughout the seven days. For even more flexibility, Weight Watchers can earn extra food by working out, using their "activity points" calculator to combine their weight with the length of time exercised and its intensity (considered high if sweating begins within five minutes) to arrive at a number indicating the food value earned. For instance, jogging for half an hour could be rewarded with an additional serving of low-fat cheese. The supposed flexibility of the Weight Watchers program is never experimental or personalized; it is formulaic and numerical, involving charts, graphs, and the implicit presence of scientific data.

I nevertheless noticed some variation within the system at the international Weight Watchers meetings I attended while travelling for research and conferences. The most striking difference was in France, where points were counted using a similar method, but bread, butter, and high-fat cheese were considered staples that could be eaten in moderation rather than avoided altogether. The meeting in Paris was held in the hastily converted breakfast room of a hotel furnished with juice machines and glass cereal dispensers filled with frosted flakes. Unlike in my Canadian town, where the mostly plumpish middle-aged women took turns sharing tips about such things as crustless pumpkin pie and Splenda-filled muffins or recounting all-you-can-eat buffet horror stories, the middle-aged women of Paris—there were actually two men, one of them clutching his wife's hand as if he were participating in a grief support group—addressed three main topics: How much chocolate should one consume? How much cheese with butter? and When should bread be eaten—in the morning, at night, or with all three meals? I was about to yell, "How about never!" in French, when the leader firmly noted that it would be both impossible and foolish to avoid these foods—the goal was not to eat 150 grams of them all at once.

Weight Watchers leaders can make such pronouncements because they are schooled in the program, and devoted to it. They must have experienced success as Weight Watchers and be lifetime members, weighing in within the requisite two pounds of their goal weight every month. The badges worn by leaders report both their first names and the total number of pounds they have lost. Regardless of location, all Weight Watchers leaders wore this badge and had a similar disposition, expressing themselves energetically and encouraging others while telling personal stories of engagement with the program. Unlike such bodybuilders as Karen Sessions, however, they did not promote experimentation with or modifications to their system; consistency and obedience were often key themes at Weight Watchers meetings. All the same, one particular leader stood out at a weekly meeting I attended in London, England, for she pushed the limits ever so slightly. As reported in my feministfiguregirl.com blog entry called "Piccadilly Circus of Sins":

> After surveying the tables spread with two-point packets of onion and cheese crisps for sale, I sat myself down with about 20 other people. Almost of all them were chubby middle-aged white women, though about two men resembling Mike Baldwin from Coronation Street before the dementia set in were also present. Oh, this will be exactly like a North American meeting, I pessimistically thought to myself, wishing I had remained in my executive suite hotel room with its daily free bottle of orange juice. But then a love-handled black female leader took the stage, and she was a breath of fresh air. In true self-help fashion, she immediately confessed to having eaten an entire apple pie in her car the day before. Audible gasps of horror echoed throughout the room. The fabulous "D" was not sorry. She defiantly explained that she had since done two spin classes to counteract her indulgent act. The energetic, pie-loving D was pro-exercise, cautioning everyone that food

discipline alone would not help them get fit. She also promoted a high-protein and veggie intake. I practically stood
up and cheered, for that is not the usual message delivered
by Weight Watchers. I pictured D savoring that cold pie by
ripping open the box and eating it with her bare hands right
off the dashboard. Obviously, I fell briefly in love with her.

This leader broke ranks by binging first and exercising later, instead
of earning her extra snack as a reward, and by unapologetically discussing her passion for apple pie. She further diverged from the
Weight Watchers doctrine by insisting that food control was not the
primary means to ensure long-term weight loss, and by promoting
protein-rich foods instead of exclusively emphasizing points values.
Like a bodybuilder, the English leader spoke from personal experience, arguing that taking pleasure in both food and intense exercise
had helped her to maintain her goal weight, a weight which she
proudly admitted was at the upper end of her height category.

Sustaining the Body

It is already clear that food is a primary concern for both bodybuilders and Weight Watchers. Yet the role of food in the two practices
diverges significantly. For bodybuilders, food is fuel that produces
the body, sending energy and nutrients to muscles in need of repair
after intensive weight lifting. Eating is encouraged, at least until one
is "on season," or within twenty weeks of a competition, when attention shifts from growing muscles to burning fat. Even while getting
bigger during their off-season, however, bodybuilders strive to "eat
clean," which involves avoiding saturated fats and excessive amounts
of refined sugar while drinking lots of water. Though opinions about
proper nutrition vary, it is standard for bodybuilders to eat at least
one or two grams of protein per pound of body weight daily. At my
off-season weight of 138 pounds, I tried to consume between 150
and 170 grams of protein every day, ideally in the form of organic
chicken breasts, lean buffalo steaks, protein powder, and egg-white
omelets. I also ate "good" carbohydrates such as sweet potatoes,
which have a low glycemic index, as well as asparagus and eggplant,
among other vegetables. Yet in truth I regularly consumed whatever

healthy foods I liked, and occasionally binged on high-sugar sweets, especially during the holidays. I gained weight without guilt or stress, believing it a necessary part of becoming more muscular.

The months leading up to a competition are, however, a different matter. During these months, a narrower array of high-protein, low-fat foods are weighed, matched with good carbohydrates, and eaten every few hours to encourage a steady metabolic rate. Food consumption is timed more carefully around a strenuous workout schedule, ensuring that the body has enough energy to burn fat, with minimal muscle loss. When on season, bodybuilders drastically increase the intensity and length of their cardio training, and often purchase such over-the-counter compounds as creatine or 1.M.R. (one more rep) to supply energy to muscles and enhance their physical performance at the gym. At the same time, the use of illegally obtained human growth hormone—artificially produced and imported from China—and various kinds of anabolic steroids as well as fat burners may be ramped up, a practice that is difficult to examine given its illegal nature. Though decried as risky by many health professionals, using banned or controlled substances is justified within the bodybuilding subculture in relation to the trusted sources of bodily knowledge previously discussed. The decision to use particular steroids, colloquially referred to as vitamin S or gear, is based on both faith in empirical (rather than only scientific) evidence and respect for the advice of experienced athletes rather than that of government officials.

During their "diet down" for a show, bodybuilders might hire coaches like Karen Sessions to guide them. These former-competitors-turned-diet-gurus follow nutritional guidelines refined through trial and error but will produce programs tailored for the individual bodies and kinds of competitions of their clients. There is no Weight Watchers "one size fits all" approach to dieting. Yet most on-season diets will involve future competitors eating the same foods over and over again, restricting them to lean chicken and one or two primary carbohydrates. This limitation of the palate undermines the connection between food and pleasure, transforming eating into a repetitive chore. When I first wrote this section of this chapter, I was consuming six daily meals that included chicken, oatmeal, protein powder, buffalo, and sweet potatoes, a menu that diminished as my competition drew nearer.

This attempt to sever food from sensuality is another striking difference between the weight-loss approach employed by body-builders and that promoted by Weight Watchers. In the corporate diet program, food is consistently presented as a pleasurable reward. The Weight Watcher demonstrates strength not by performing heavier dead lifts but by practicing self-control in relation to food, indulging in it reasonably to achieve either a delayed or partial grati-fication. Exercise is undertaken rather paradoxically by the con-formist Weight Watcher; exercise does not transform food into a muscular body but "removes" food from the body by burning up cal-ories, and thus earning the right to eat more food. In this sense, food is always a treat for the obedient Weight Watcher who, like a pure-bred dog at the Westminster dog show, is motivated to demonstrate good behavior in the anticipation of future tidbits. Of course, this consistently measured interaction with food is difficult to sustain, even for a lifetime member, leading Cressida Heyes to suggest that failure and subsequent weight regain is an essential though unspo-ken part of the Weight Watchers regime, creating an endless supply of loyal clients who rejoin the program.[30]

Most bodybuilders also typically fail to uncouple food from pleasure, and are occasionally rewarded with a cheat meal, in part to stave off cravings and provide some mental relief from hardcore diet-ing, but also to restore glycogen to tired muscles and boost a sluggish metabolism. Some competitive bodybuilders sustain their rigid diets by dreaming of a future cheat meal, similar to rewards earned in the Weight Watchers system, and almost all of them look forward to a postcontest pig-out meal. Such binging is featured in the *Pumping Iron* films, both I and II, in which male and female athletes jubilantly share cheesecake and other forbidden delicacies backstage.[31] Many bodybuilders at the Canadian nationals in 2010—I was there to sup-port a friend who was competing—ordered such high-fat foods as pizza and lasagna after the final show, while discussing the pancakes and waffles they planned to have for breakfast. I nevertheless parted ways with the reverence paid to the IHOP (International House of Pancakes) by a surprising number of bodybuilders, for I planned to savor my cheat meals in Lebanese and Ethiopian restaurants.

Unlike the ideally static Weight Watchers body, which achieves and then maintains a goal weight, the built body is unstable. It gets larger as it bulks up during the off-season and then leans out before competitions. On one hand there is much to recommend this cyclical approach, for it recognizes that the body is always changing, and makes continual adjustments, while understanding food as a crucial part of physical existence rather than an indulgence. In contrast, Weight Watchers promotes the ideal of an impossibly stable body, apparently unaffected by aging, stress, hormonal cycles, or injury, while framing food as a luxurious temptation that must be either resisted or earned. On the other hand, it is difficult to portray the built body as a reasonable one, especially when considering the extreme conditioning sought by competitive bodybuilders, notably those in the light-, middle-, and heavyweight classes. After witnessing my friend's participation in the Canadian national competition, I wrote a blog entry called "Bodybuilder's Bitch," describing the experience:

> Picture a standard hotel room at the Hilton, with two double beds facing a flat-screen TV. Brown stains cover a rumpled sheet that lies across the narrow entrance hallway. A heavyweight female bodybuilder stands on top of it, wearing only a g-string, arms outspread. Two women kneel on either side of her, spraying her skin with tanning lotion, smoothing the smears with a small foam brush. "I am going to open your ass crack now to paint inside it," says one of the worker bees. "Your baby monkey butt," jokes the other prone woman, for she is something of a smart aleck. "Just do it," sighs the exhausted, dehydrated, ripped, and increasingly dark brown bodybuilder. "Treat me like an object." The two painters shuffle the sculpted object into the bathroom to eye her from all sides, deciding that the "side body"—as yoga types would say—needs some attention during the next application. They pause to let the 6th coat dry by watching a compelling scene from *Thelma and Louise*.
>
> It was a strangely intimate and perversely feminist event. I was the smart-alecky one, helping my friend prepare to compete in the Canadian Bodybuilding Championships, held this year in Saskatoon. The temporary object-woman is an amazing athlete who had trained hard all year, dieted down to a mere 135 pounds, and then water loaded before restricting liquids for two days and finally fat loading. Such

competition preparation is banal to those in the bodybuilding world, but it was eye opening to a neophyte like me. I
had baked cheesecakes for the fat load: one was banana with
a blueberry swirl and the other chocolate with a cinnamon
nut crust. They were fab, if I do say so myself. After consuming bland chicken and egg whites for months on end,
my muscular amiga was finally allowed to eat mixed nuts,
peanut butter, cake, and rib-eye steaks—but without any
appetite or hydration, she said that it all tasted like "ass."

This kind of stage preparation is not only physically draining but
can promote both long-term eating disorders and a perpetual dissat-
isfaction with the body as it approaches, but never quite reaches, its
desired state of perfection.

So far my discussion of sustaining the body has not included
yoga. This is not surprising since diet seems to have little to do with
yoga (except when students are training to become yoga instructors), and the topic was never broached in any class that I took. A
quick online search for "yoga diet" nevertheless produced a few sites
describing the Ayurvedic diet, a traditional Indian way of eating that
is individualized, based on each person's temperament, as well as
on such factors as the season.[32] Resembling to a certain degree the
humoral system informing early modern conceptions of nourishment, the Ayurvedic diet strives to achieve balance and unity with
the environment, not muscle gain or fat loss.[33] Balance and unity
were indeed themes in my hatha classes, but we considered them
in relation to breathing rather than food. Various instructors would
request that we close our eyes and concentrate on respiration, feeling our breath move up and down our spines while experiencing the
materiality of the air and rendering it palpable all around us. One
yoga teacher noted that while we paid great attention to food and
water, we typically failed to appreciate the life-giving nature of the
breath, encouraging us to be mindful of our breathing and to breathe
audibly by relaxing our throats while sucking in and out that essential air.

My personal trainer always reminds me to breathe during our
back and leg sessions at the gym. She has me inhale while lowering or retracting, and then exhale during an explosive lift or push.

Instead of creating yogic stillness or a new sense of embodied being, this breathing technique provides energy and momentum to forceful movement. In bodybuilding, the breath is a tool that can be applied mechanically. Like food, the breath is a kind of external fuel that is internalized and used to get a better pump. Yogic breathing is not entirely different, as the breath is recognized and directed, sent sometimes to sore or stiff body parts. Yet the focused breathing we practiced during my yoga classes was also about locating oneself in the world, and feeling part of it. This sort of reflective breathing is not central to bodybuilding, or at least not for me.

In contrast to the continual attention paid to the breath in both bodybuilding and yoga, there is no talk whatsoever about breathing in the Weight Watchers program. There is, however, quite a bit of hot air expelled at the meetings when members describe their successes and failures during the previous week or exchange tips on how to resist Halloween treats by putting down the mini Mars bar and picking up a bowl of fresh fruit topped with one tablespoon of sugar-free chocolate sauce. This talk is labeled "support" by the Weight Watchers corporation and is considered one of the four pillars of weight loss, along with behavior, food, and exercise. According to their website, "many people who have achieved sustained weight-loss with Weight Watchers tell us that they believe attending the meetings was the single biggest reason that they were successful."[34] In keeping with its self-help basis, the Weight Watchers program creates a community of dieters, mostly women, who confess to cheating and are then forgiven by the group, or who listen to others and applaud their weight-loss announcements or avowals to start some low-level fitness activity such as walking.

When I rejoined Weight Watchers after moving to a new city, these meetings were my favorite part of the process. Having left behind a strong feminist community, I welcomed the chance to interact with a range of women, most of whom were not academics. These encounters were often amusing and could be empowering. Some of the lessons have even stayed with me, including one leader's assertion that "Just because you stumble on one step does not mean that you should throw yourself down the rest of the stairs. Pick yourself up and keep going." Yet according to sociologist Heidi Rimke, self-help doctrine is paradoxical, as it directs adherents to follow the advice of authorities even as it stresses individual agency.[35] This focus can emphasize individual responsibility in a way that negates the broader social context. In Weight Watchers, everyone is personally accountable for weight gain or loss, and broader pressures to consume constantly while maintaining a thin, "feminine" form are never addressed. According to Rimke, this narrow self-help message ultimately produces manageable liberal subjects focused on self-care rather than political critique, a point confirmed by Heyes in her analysis of both the appeal and danger of the Weight Watchers' mantra.[36]

A different kind of community is formed at my yoga classes, which are often attended by the same group of people, most of them women. The sense of community is, however, founded on shared physical practice, not talking. In fact, silent meditation is the preferred preclass activity, and we tend to leave quietly, perhaps exchanging only a nod or wave. My bodybuilding practice rests somewhere in between the role of talk involved in Weight Watchers and its absence from yoga, with bouts of intense physicality interspersed with chatty conversation. My personal trainer regularly encourages me while I focus intently on the task at hand, using words to supply me with the energy required to perform one more chest press as my muscles begin to fail, or to instruct me to keep my core tight during the last few dead lifts. Although these positive affirmations are more specific than those given at Weight Watchers meetings, they contribute to creating a community at the gym, one that is based on emotional support between women as well as on the exchange of practical information related to growing muscle and losing fat. Some scholars criticize the competitive nature of bodybuilding, arguing that it pits women against each other, but this has not been my experience. On the contrary, I adore both my current and previous trainer, and try to relate to women of all fitness levels at the gym, striking up conversations and "gym friendships" with them. These friendships can extend beyond the gym proper, including road trips to Las Vegas or simply weekend plans to meet for coffee. My decision to enter a competition has only extended this network of supportive women, and this community is one reason why working out at the gym is often the highlight of my day, something I consider more fully in Chapter Three.

Conclusions

It is likely obvious that I relish bodybuilding, respect the practice of hatha yoga, and have an ambivalent attitude toward Weight Watchers. These responses are based on first-hand experiences with each activity, though I know less about yoga than I do about working out with weights or counting points alongside fellow Weight Watchers. This comparison has nevertheless revealed important areas of overlap and distinction between the three practices, ultimately providing a more thorough and specific conception of the built body. This body is indeed a mechanical one, understood as a fleshly machine that can become objectified, subject to the evaluating gaze of oneself and others. It is furthermore goal driven, always striving to become stronger, faster, harder. Yet the built body is also unstable and arguably unattainable, potentially existing only in pre- and postcompetition photographs. Though engaged in a rigid cyclical regime, the built body is not simply forced to conform to an ideal shape. In the end, there is no single ideal or norm, and each body remains unique. This diversity continues because bodybuilding is a fully embodied practice in which the body itself is a primary source of knowledge, with its authority based on extensive periods of self-experimentation translated into visibly distinctive results that are admired by a supportive community of people engaged in the same endeavor.

There is surprisingly little overlap between the physical techniques of the built body and those involved in the Weight Watchers program. Whereas the built body is assessed visually and experienced physically, the Weight Watcher is disembodied, transformed into numbers, and evaluated in relation to an average. Though this normalized body is similarly goal driven, it is meant to get smaller, reach an ideal, and then stay the same forever. The body of the Weight Watcher is not a source of knowledge—it is subject to knowledge, part of a system that is designed and regularly updated by outside experts. Weight Watchers receive support from a community of dieters and follow rules provided by authorities in order to take personal responsibility for achieving and then sustaining conformity, controlling food as well as their emotional responses to food.

Both practices might seem utterly at odds with yoga, which is not goal driven or about control but rather involves broader conceptions of the relationship between mind, body, and spirit. While it is true that yoga and the Weight Watchers regime have little in common, there are some interesting links between yoga and bodybuilding. Even as the yoga body is not visually evaluated, compared with others, or dieted to become bigger or smaller, the practice of yoga is fundamentally embodied, highlighting intense forms of physicality in order to learn from the body. Like the built body, this engaged form of embodiment is always changing, and is unique to each individual. There are no norms to achieve, but there is a searching for improvement and contentment that accords with my experience and observations of bodybuilding.

This comparison sets the stage for the next chapter, in which I consider the experience of lifting weights in more detail, drawing on phenomenological theories of embodiment in order to analyze the sensation of muscle failure. The discussion above provides the necessary introduction to this bodybuilding subculture, including its particular argot, way of viewing the body, and often supportive community. Instead of generalizing about the contemporary fitness culture, it foregrounds the specificities of bodybuilding while undermining the stereotypes often associated with it, namely its assertion of mastery and pursuit of pain. As the rest of this book will show, bodybuilding often involves self-care, a quest for personal knowledge, and a nurturing community, for male as well as female participants. I will insist that bodybuilding does not inhibit physical transcendence, but rather promotes it, moving practitioners through materiality, into the unknown.

TWO

Embodiment and the Event of Muscle Failure

"Matter means that at any given moment, not everything is possible."[1]
—Maurice Merleau-Ponty

A camera frames the face, neck, and shoulder caps of a figure who begins to do overhead machine presses, repeatedly pushing weights upward. The tops of the shoulders gradually flex more slowly, and signs of increasing effort mark the athlete's face, complete with parted lips, clenched jaw, and involuntary blinking. The featured shoulder muscles quiver, and then finally freeze. As the weights heavily drop, the exhausted exerciser exhales and laughs with delight, face relaxing. A voice-over asserts: "Exercise changes your life. This is what I believe." In this short video, entitled "Who is Heather Cassils?," a studied loss of physical control, otherwise known as muscle failure, is linked with transformation and elation. This video can be found on YouTube.

The idea that exercise can alter your body and identity is common in contemporary consumer culture, which often presents working out as a disciplined form of self-improvement. Yet this superficial understanding of getting fitter and therefore better by conforming to a physical ideal—currently a lean, somewhat muscular body for women—is not Cassils's message. As both a professional fitness instructor and an accomplished visual artist, with an MFA from the California Institute of the Arts, Cassils has a versatile approach to the human body, informed by critical theory, historical knowledge, and a comprehension of physiology.[2] Some of Cassils's internationally recognized art works, which center on feats of physical endurance and the display of trans identity, are analyzed in Chapter Four, but here I want to focus on the promotional YouTube video mentioned above. In this video, the trainer presents both a persona and a product. Written text overlapping the images of Cassils working out explains: "I combine empathy, humor, intelligence, knowledge, and motivation." The personal trainer goes on to promise creative, diverse, and challenging sessions that will "push people," warning viewers and possible customers that getting fit requires effort. One of Cassils's assertions—"you have to break things down to build things up"—refers most directly to the technique of muscle failure, which involves training to the point of momentary muscle exhaustion, such as doing shoulder presses until the engaged muscles lack the strength to complete another repetition and literally cease to function.[3] Although its value is debated, this maneuver is commonly used by bodybuilders to recruit all of their muscle fibers at once, pushing both the fast- and slow-twitch fibers to their limit, and thereby stimulating the muscle to respond to increased demand by growing bigger.[4] Roughly speaking, the failing muscles are flooded with lactic acid, stressed, and "damaged," compelling them to regenerate.

In the video, Cassils positions deliberate muscle exhaustion as the foundation of athletic and other capacities. The steady close-up shots of the trainer's pursuit of muscle failure are interspersed with more lively scenes that show Cassils boxing, doing hammer curls with heavy dumbbells, and undertaking athletic stunts. Unlike the comparably static views of the shoulder workout described above, these clips reveal Cassils's entire body in motion, engaging with both objects and people—sometimes while clad in a t-shirt that declares "Chicks Pump Iron." According to the visual logic and verbal messages of Cassils's video, it is this initial and even monotonous breaking down of the body that enables its subsequent bursts of energetic movement. Restraint allows freedom; failure leads to success.

Few philosophical approaches to embodiment embrace a similar attitude. Most of them understand movement as crucial to the production of bodily awareness and a sense of the lived body, arguing that physical restraint is at odds with freedom. Supporters of the feminist theories of the body discussed below, for example, would no doubt rate the images that portray Cassils actively intervening

in various situations as more positive representations of embodiment than the close-cropped shot of the face and neck with which
the video begins. The clips of Cassils running, jumping, and lifting
appear robustly to challenge gendered norms by highlighting subjectivity as the personal trainer declares himself a "chick" able to do
"manly" things. In contrast, the tight framing of Cassils's made-up,
symmetrical, and attractive visage recalls the conventions of a fashion magazine cover, mimicking a standardized portrayal of beauty.
While in some ways the effort eventually written on Cassils's face
breaks with the traditionally blank canvas of the fashion model,
serving to humanize the trainer, in other ways the shoulder press
segments of "Who is Heather Cassils?" objectify the protagonist,
separating face from body, and offering the former up for scrutiny.[5]
Yet I contend that Cassils's video is subversive when it portrays the
experience of muscle failure as a groundbreaking corporeal situation.
By foregrounding a material body that can be trained but never fully
controlled, it reveals that a simultaneous striving for and lack of control is a crucial part of bodybuilding and its pleasures.

This chapter is about the radical potential of muscle failure.
Though I have begun with a discussion of Cassils's video, and will
return to it in my conclusions, I explore this theme primarily in relation to my own experience of lifting weights to failure, focusing on
a detailed account of my "first time." I also refer to a few anecdotal
accounts of weight training provided to me by female bodybuilders
and power lifters, stressing the elements in their stories that overlap with and diverge from my own. In the first section I situate my
methodology within a wider historiography of scholarly analyses
of female athletes, especially those that draw on forms of feminist
phenomenology to elucidate the topic. I argue that their reliance on
phenomenological principles, drawn primarily from French philosopher Maurice Merleau-Ponty and the subsequent expansion of his
work to include considerations of gender by such feminist thinkers
as Simone de Beauvoir and Iris Marion Young, can offer enlight-
ening ways to grasp the experience of muscle failure and what it
might mean in contemporary culture. I nevertheless take issue with
how practically all of these accounts, both past and present, privilege
movement at the expense of stasis. They thereby risk idealizing the
stereotypically masculine pursuit of vigorous action while overlooking other forms of embodied being or physical knowledge. By means

of an analysis of muscle failure, I unorthodoxly assert that experiencing a motionless body, or else a body that unsuccessfully strives for motion, can in some circumstances be important for women.

Failing Female Athletes

In their survey of critical writing on the sociocultural aspects of women's exercise, sport researchers Eileen Kennedy and Pirkko Markula argue that most studies either analyze media depictions of fit bodies, or describe how participants have actually experienced different kinds of physical activity.[6] Scholars who examine representations of athletic women in contemporary Western culture conclude that many images reproduce heteronormativity by feminizing women's physical activities, uniformly promoting a body that is thin, toned, and young, appealing to a straight male audience. This aesthetic ideal is equated with beauty and health—the two are indistinguishable—and all women are tasked with pursuing it as an individual responsibility that is at once conscientiously devoted to disease prevention and personally empowering. Critics claim that the current emphasis on finding freedom, happiness, and fulfillment in the achievement of fitness and weight loss draws on feminist rhetoric, subverting it to promote a kind of self-actualization that is really about becoming increasingly docile, malleable, and productive within a postcapitalist marketplace.[7] Intentionally or not, fitness experts and health providers collude in shaping a version of commodity feminism that many women are eager to buy.

In contrast, research focused on women's lived experience of physical activity tends to use such qualitative methods as participant observation and unstructured interviews, striving to reveal women's direct accounts of working out in local gyms, aerobics classes, or while jogging outside rather than emphasizing visual representations of fitness. These scholars find that even as the majority of women admittedly train in pursuit of an ideal body image and wish to lose weight, they are not simply oppressed by the dominant forms of Western popular culture. Women discover ways to negotiate and resist prevailing messages, sometimes by highlighting the female camaraderie of an aerobics class rather than pursuing the femininely toned look such exercise is supposed to create.[8] Along similar lines, a recent study by Samantha Holland uses ethnographic and survey methods to consider the current pole-dancing fitness craze, which teaches women to mimic the movements of performers in a strip club by climbing on and swinging from what is popularly known as a "stripper's pole," ostensibly to develop upper-body and core strength.[9] Holland concludes that while amateur pole dancers typically dislike traditional forms of exercise, they enjoy this energetic erotic dancing, which allows them to express their sexuality in a rather conventional but safe manner—men are not allowed to be present during classes—while reporting increased feelings of physical power and strength that can liberate them from gendered norms.

Despite including the diverse voices of real women, such research about female athleticism has some limitations. It tends to convey narrative accounts of exercise instead of in-depth analyses of women's embodied experience. There are relatively few investigations of what it feels like to work out, probably because it is difficult to access the physicality of this experience without resorting to and reiterating the dominant cultural understandings of bodies and gender. An interest in arriving at a more complete account of women's differing forms of embodiment is nevertheless paramount in a wide range of intellectual endeavors, notably historical accounts. In her work on eighteenth-century Germany, historian Barbara Duden, for instance, mines the case notes recorded by Doctor Johann Storch to argue that his female clients perceived their bodies in terms of the healthy exchange of fluids and unhealthy occurrence of "stoppages" or hardenings.[10] Duden explains that she had to overcome her commonsense understandings of the human body, informed by modern medical and scientific theories, to recognize an early modern body that was composed of four shifting humors and fundamentally open to the world, continually interacting with such forces as temperature, humidity, gusting winds, and moving planets, among other things. This body was not yet a machine made up of functioning parts, nor a fortress in need of protection from threatening external elements.[11]

Scholars concerned with contemporary aspects of female embodiment likewise make efforts to think differently and set assumptions aside, however temporarily. A number of feminist theorists have pursued this goal, striving to grasp "matters themselves" in the "world as it is experienced," by engaging with the key concepts inspired by phenomenology, typically responding to the work of French philosopher Maurice Merleau-Ponty, himself influenced by the so-called father of phenomenology, Edmund Husserl.[12] Husserl diverged from philosophical tradition by arguing that knowledge is based on lived experience and advocating the method of "phenomenological reduction," which deliberately suspends the belief that the things we see really exist to consider only the experience we have of them.[13] The point is to produce careful, prereflective descriptions of phenomena as they appear—"letting things be seen in the manner in which they show themselves"—and as they are meaningful to an experiencing subject. Although this process requires a first-person account of how the world appears to the person describing it, the end result is to create a tension between the universal and the unique, exploring the possibility that the particular experience in question could shed light on broader concepts. In one case study, Husserl looked at a coffee cup, noting that it had to be physically turned in order to be seen from the back, after having been viewed from the front, top, and sides.[14] He concluded that objects never show themselves from all angles at once, a perception that holds for any organism but also suggests that nothing can be immediately perceived or fully known. Yet attending to what he called *Leib*, or the lived body, instead of a more biologically or psychologically understood corporeal entity, was only one of Husserl's major philosophical contributions, and such experts as Sara Heinämaa have examined how Husserl later developed his ideas to explore, among other things, the precise role played by the ego in generating psychic acts, ultimately positing the existence of a pure or transcendental ego.[15]

Some philosophers inspired by Husserl's theories nevertheless criticize what they consider his commitment to a stance of disinterest and quiet contemplation in the face of an object. Merleau-Ponty, for example, adopted the method of reduction, wishing to consider "just what is given" in experience, but joined others in arguing that the phenomenological reduction is neither pure nor complete. Expanding on Husserl's conception of an embodied consciousness, the French philosopher affirmed that the lived body is a fundamental structure of human existence, perceiving a world filled with opportunities for action, and thus inseparable from it. In her summary of Merleau-Ponty's ideas, Komarine Romdenh-Romluc explains that "What a perceiver sees on any particular occasion is the result of what she can do, where this depends on both the nature of her surroundings, and her capacities for action."[16] The categories of perception and action are "two sides of the same ability to engage with the world," which pulls us toward investing it with values. Rejecting the notion of a transcendental ego, Merleau-Ponty argued that action is expressive, and that all expressions are forms of thought. Thinking is thus embodied, rather than located in a distinctive mind, and the body is itself a type of subjectivity.[17]

Alongside her colleague Merleau-Ponty, French feminist philosopher Simone de Beauvoir drew from and developed the foundational work of Husserl, though she critiqued the way in which both men recognized sexual difference but nonetheless presumed a male body in their accounts of embodied experience. The diverse scholarly and literary publications of Beauvoir, which ultimately employ an interdisciplinary methodology, have sometimes been labeled as empirical or socio-psychological studies of the construction of gender, but Heinämaa has recently revealed Beauvoir's fundamental engagement with and contribution to phenomenology.[18] According to Heinämaa, the most famous and arguably most influential work by Beauvoir, *The Second Sex*, first published in 1949, is primarily concerned with the "ambiguity of the lived body and its dual expressions, the feminine and the masculine."[19] Instead of merely either revealing the oppression of women as "other" or condemning modern forms of feminine behavior, Beauvoir "formulates gender as a corporeal locus of cultural possibilities both received and innovated."[20] In Judith Butler's reading of *The Second Sex*, gender is a way of existing one's body, with the body understood as a "situation, or a field of cultural possibilities both received and reinterpreted."[21] Living gender is an endless and ongoing project even as it is not simply chosen from limitless possibilities. Toward the end of *The Second Sex*, Beauvoir describes the female experience of activities formerly overlooked or taken for granted, including motherhood and housework, but goes beyond Husserl by evaluating them along ethical lines, calling for women to pursue emancipation in the choices made during their everyday lives.[22] Beauvoir's innovative and wide-ranging interest in the particularities of female embodiment and her political commitment to changing women's position by reshaping gendered bodies was and remains a groundbreaking source for continuing feminist phenomenological research.

Probably the most cited work in this tradition is "Throwing Like a Girl," an essay published by political scientist Iris Marion Young in 1989. She combines the insights of Merleau-Ponty and Beauvoir to argue that the imposition of gender norms compromise women's free movement to produce a specific kind of feminine bodily comportment. According to Young, a woman's relation to her body is hesitant because she simultaneously experiences it as a thing and a capacity, whereas men tend to comprehend their bodies as the originators of motion rather than subject to it. Women, for instance, will throw a ball awkwardly and with restraint, in telling contrast to the full-bodied and more forceful manner achieved by many men. Paying attention to how bodies are lived in space, Young contends that women

> experience our bodies as a fragile encumbrance, rather than the media for the enactment of our aims. We feel as though we must have our attention directed upon our bodies to make sure they are doing what we wish them to do, rather than paying attention to what we want to do through our bodies. [23]

Young's generalizations refer to how women are taught to mistrust the abilities of their bodies, viewing them as things on display rather than modes of accomplishment. She concludes that any woman who lives her body as a thing is unable to engage freely in the world's possibilities.

Feminists have been both inspired by and quick to criticize Young's study of women's physical experience of space and movement, finding counter examples. Analyses of the physical accomplishments of women who undertake such activities as martial arts training, spin classes, Pilates, and rock climbing are offered as evidence that Young's claims, based on observations made during the 1970s and 1980s, are outdated. Literary critic Dianne Chisholm, for example, elaborates on the vivid descriptions provided by female mountaineer Lynn Hill, who has "free climbed" some of the world's most formidable mountains without using ropes or tools, moving her body in ways that are hardly timid, hesitant, or inhibited.[24] According to Chisholm and other writers, a wide range of female athletes perform swift, embodied movements that expand their interaction with the world, despite the male domination of the particular fields in question and the wider patriarchal structures liable to contain women.

This new emphasis on the limitless possibilities of women's activity is heartening but continues to insist that physical motion should be unencumbered, directed upward and outward. Feminist scholars assume that women engaged in free motion are in effect pursuing freedom. They portray unrestrained physical movement as itself a feminist act with the potential to liberate all women. In contrast, women who move in self-conscious, objectified, or restricted ways can only be unethically devoted to reinforcing the gendered status quo, contributing to the disciplining and even punishment of all women. Bluntly stated, on these terms participating in a figure or bodybuilding competition is an antifeminist act, whereas running a marathon or climbing a mountain are feminist acts. Wishing to expose as well as unsettle such presumptions, I now turn to a careful assessment of the deliberate and restrained bodily stasis that is produced by lifting weights to failure.

Embracing the Limits of Matter

I sat on a small, black chair with a short back, faced the expansive mirrored wall in front of me, gripped a pair of dumbbells, and proceeded to do shoulder presses. Starting with a weight in each hand, held beside my shoulders, I lifted the weights overhead in unison. By the fourth set of repetitions, I had fifteen pounds in each hand, a light load that now makes me laugh. My trainer was encouraging me with shouts of "keep going," while counting my repetitions. Suddenly my arms froze in midpress. My brain kept telling them to move. I commanded, "Push you lazy bitches," but my senseless shoulders did not comply. I looked in noncomprehension at my trainer, and she just laughed. With the slightest assistance, she helped me to raise the weights, shakily, one last time before explaining the physiology of my current situation and its role in promoting muscle growth by pushing the body to its limit.

From that point on I was addicted, pursuing failure whenever possible, without overtraining—that is, overworking my muscles by neglecting to allow them time to rest and regenerate. I loved the instance of failure, which made my body materially present, as an active agent that was both me and not-me. I experienced a body that was not entirely under my control, defying my imagination of a supposedly separate mind that sent messages through a nervous system. I savored how difficult it was to predict precisely when failure would occur. On some days I was tired and failed quickly; on other days, I had eaten more or slept longer and could lift heavier weights for extended periods. I nevertheless came to recognize the signs of impending failure, which often included visible twitching at the muscle site, as well as a certain inner tension and heat that would gather inside the site before all sensation stopped. Overall, my self-image was transformed. I came to understand my body as a palpable fleshliness with a will of its own; it was at once unmanageable and agreeable to getting bigger and stronger as I wished it to do.

My attempt to convey this experience in words is another instance of failure. I am unable to produce a "pure" phenomenological account of it, following the method of Husserl, without making assumptions or bringing values to the event. Husserl himself often mentioned concrete examples in passing, such as his encounter with a coffee cup, without fully analyzing them, being more intent on formulating a methodology than practicing it. His conclusion that objects do not show themselves from all sides at once is only partly applicable to my own example of failed shoulder muscles. During the shoulder press incident, my upper body was frozen; it was an unresponsive "thing" subject to the gaze. In some ways, objectification or at least an increased self-consciousness are crucial aspects of bodybuilding. Before any kind of training begins, the body is visually evaluated, and this observation continues unabated during workouts. It is necessary for bodybuilders to regard their muscles continually, watching for proper form and technique, especially during a repetition, as discussed in the previous chapter. This deliberate distancing from the body is enhanced by mirrors, which constantly reflect an image of the bodybuilder back to him- or herself. Watching my body during the moment of muscle failure was unlike looking at a coffee cup, as I was able to see all sides of the object (my body) both because of the mirrors surrounding me and my trainer, who extended my eyes by observing my form, ready to intervene when required.

Husserl was well aware that the body is never simply an object comparable to other objects. He considered the problem of the perceiving body, arguing that "The same body that serves me as a means of all perception stands in my way in the perception of itself and is a remarkably incompletely constituted thing."[25] In an essay called "Objective Reality, Spatial Orientation, and the Body," written around 1913, and finally published as part of *Ideas II* in 1952, Husserl explores how the body perceives itself perceiving:

> Obviously, the Body is also to be seen just like any other thing, but it becomes a Body only by incorporating tactile sensations, pain sensations, etc.—in short, by the localization of the sensations as sensations.[26]

According to Husserl, the eye does not appear visually—that is, the eye can never see itself seeing. A mirrored reflection does not expose the act of perception itself. And, just as visual sensations are not located in the eyes, so too in hearing "the ear is 'there,' but the sensed tone is not localized in the ear."[27] Using the example of one hand touching the other, Husserl argues that the body can nevertheless feel itself feel, making the tactile sense the ground for body self-awareness. There the body, perceived by means of the body, is the corporeal body itself:

> Touching my left hand, I have touch-appearance, that is to say, I do not just sense, but I perceive and have appearances of a soft, smooth hand, with such a form. The indicational sensations of movement and the representational sensations of touch, which are Objectified as features of the thing, "left hand," belong in fact to my right hand. But when I touch the left hand I also find in it, too, series of touch-sensations, which are "*localized*" in it, though these are not constitutive of properties (such as roughness or smoothness of the hand, of this physical thing). If I speak of the *physical* thing, "left hand," then I am abstracting from these sensations (a ball of lead has nothing like them and likewise for every "merely" physical thing, every thing that is not my Body). If I do include them, then it is not that the physical thing is now richer, but instead *it becomes Body, it senses.*[28]

Husserl contends that the body is perceived by localized tactile sensations, with the lived body essentially understood as the "bearer of sensations."

This approach to embodiment is appealing in many ways, especially for its emphasis on touch instead of vision, at odds with a long history of ocularcentrism (the privileging of vision over the other senses) in Western philosophy and theology.[29] Yet the approach seems to imply a body that is bounded by skin as a form or shape, restricted by the perception of tactile sensations. This enclosed body does not help me to think about the experience of muscle failure. For in that situation my body was extended, by the chair in which I was sitting, the dumbbells I was holding, and my trainer, who stood behind me, initially replacing my eyes and then supporting my failed shoulder muscles. Nor is the experience of muscle failure a sensation per se; it is more accurately described as a lack of sensation, a sudden halt to bodily communication, or a surprising blankness.[30] When I was performing multiple overhead shoulder presses, for instance, I had felt an intense pressure and warming that could be expressed as a kind of touching or inner sense of tactility, but the ensuing few seconds of failure were senseless, leading to a sudden disconnect from my body, or at least some parts of it, making it seem less like a body and more like a recalcitrant thing.

Despite depending to a certain degree on Husserl's claims, Merleau-Ponty introduced ideas that more helpfully shed light on the experience of muscle failure, suggesting why it might initially have been a shocking and memorable event for me. The differences between how the two men theorized the body have been thoroughly explored by Professor of Philosophy Taylor Carman in an article highlighting Merleau-Ponty's arguments about what he called the body schema. I find this particular notion difficult to grasp for it has nothing to do with popular discussions of body image and is instead informed by a kind of Kantian schematism, positing an *a priori* condition of cognition. Taylor explains that the body schema is a preconceptual motor intentionality that manifests itself in the perceptual body.[31] In other words, the body is never a passive receptor of sensations, or reducible to flesh itself, but is more fundamentally understood in terms of capacities that predict and structure our awareness of objects. Taylor argues that for Merleau-Ponty the body schema is "an integrated set of skills poised and ready to anticipate and incorporate a world prior to the application of concepts and the formation of thoughts and judgments."[32] Merleau-Ponty contends that the body "exists towards its tasks," meaning that we learn about it, acquiring what Husserl would call the lived body, by actively taking up bodily possibilities.

Although it is rather challenging to think about something that pre-exists cognition, Merleau-Ponty's construction of the body schema becomes clearer and more convincing with reference to examples. Consider the fascinating case of so-called phantom limbs, when someone who has lost an arm or a leg through amputation or accident nevertheless vividly feels pain and other sensations in the missing appendage.[33] According to the theory of the body schema, such an experience is not simply delusional or the result of disordered thinking. It is caused by the continuing effect of the sufferer's body schema—that is, of his or her longstanding sense of what the body can and cannot do. Phantom limbs are temporary; the affected person will eventually alter his or her body schema, not through the sheer force of will or by means of deliberate reflection but by acquiring a new orientation to the world. Over time, his or her habitual body schema will adjust to one more appropriate to the actual body. The body schema is thus dynamic; it is an "established perceptual background against which [we] perceive and respond to changes and movements in [our] environment."[34]

Merleau-Ponty's theories have been taken up by feminist scholars because they can be expanded to explain gendered experiences of space and embodiment without essentializing male or female bodies, equating the body with material flesh, or erasing historical and cultural differences in bodily experience. Iris Marion Young draws on the concept of the body schema to argue that instead of experiencing the world in terms of "I can"—that is, as oriented toward certain projects based on bodily capacities—women often experience an "I cannot" inhibition of intentionality. While she highlights the restrained female body, I have already described how other scholars emphasize the opportunities that increasingly exist for women to live multiple kinds of bodies—freer bodies, they would contend—by undertaking assertive, expansive movements during such activities as mountain climbing. Yet, as far as I know, the concept of body schema has not been applied to research on bodybuilding, and certainly not to the pursuit of muscle failure. It is nevertheless useful, for my first experience of muscle failure created a sudden and unexpected disarticulation of my body which, though in a manner less drastic than amputation, disrupted my body schema. This disruption was

initially shocking, but as my weight training and experience of muscle failure became habitual, my body schema recalibrated, ultimately
changing my experience of space as well as my thought processes,
scholarly research goals, and orientation to the world in general. In
contrast to the values promoted in most if not all feminist versions
of phenomenology, my altered body schema stemmed from the "I
cannot" experience of restraint and a rather passive lack of sensation,
if not exactly from a thorough objectification of my body, which can
never fully occur within the terms outlined by Merleau-Ponty. Still,
my defining moment was anything but dynamic, and it shifted my
attention to my body as a type of matter for which "not everything
is possible."

After my intense and arguably liberating encounter with muscle
failure, I sought other limit experiences, wanting to test what my
body could not do or become. Among other things, I decided to diet
and train seriously for a figure competition, a challenge described in
subsequent chapters. This reference to limit experiences deliberately
invokes the work of Michel Foucault, with which I have engaged for
years in contrast to my more recent investigation of phenomenological theories. Inspired by such writers as Georges Bataille, Foucault was fascinated by extreme experiences, such as madness and
suffering, able to wrest the subject from itself, exposing its lack of
unity.[35] Though Foucault's later writing on the history of sexuality
does not employ the phrase "limit experience," subsequent highly
controversial biographies have recounted the philosopher's pursuit of
novel sensations in sadomasochist practices and anonymous sexual
encounters before his death.[36] Although my experience of muscle
failure was unaccompanied by pain—indeed by any tactile sensation—and was for me a kind of limit experience, I concurrently had
other, more sensational experiences at the gym that reoriented my
body, if not as dramatically. For instance, while lifting heavy weights
or breaking a sweat in an arduous spin class, I often became overwhelmed by endorphin rushes, whereby my body was suffused
with a morphine-like substance from within.[37] Scientifically speaking, endorphins are peptides released by the pituitary gland during
intense exercise or pain, as well as during orgasm. In fitness culture,
an endorphin rush is a gratifying reward for hard work or "good
suffering," providing a sudden feeling of well-being associated with
surpassing a physical limit. The link between endorphins and release

or sexual pleasure, familiar to many exercisers, including me, was recently explored in a quantitative research study that showed that many women have exercise-induced orgasms or erotic feelings at the gym, especially while repetitively performing abdominal- and core-strengthening movements.[38] This response can be explained in physiological terms, as the result of pelvic contractions, but can also be related to the kind of limit experience that pushes the body beyond conventional boundaries, encouraging its surrender. These less extreme examples of pleasure rather than pain (or of pain transformed into pleasure) could illustrate Foucault's insistence that the "rallying point for the counterattack against the deployment of sexuality ought not to be sexual desire, but rather the body and pleasure."[39] Because endorphin rushes are diffuse, involving the entire surface of the body rather than only sexualized body parts, and do not emanate from the desire of one person toward another person or an object, they might undermine the normalizing effects of current discursive constructions of sexuality. Overall, then, intense exercise offers multiple possibilities for reshaping human bodies and, in certain cases, even the body schema.

This discussion does not suggest that all women would be similarly affected by the experiences of muscle failure and endorphin rushes. When I randomly asked fitness friends at the gym, including several competitive bodybuilders, about their first instance of muscle failure, all of them recalled it vividly. A few remarked that it was a turning point, after which they were addicted to weight lifting, but others were less impressed by the experience. Most interesting to me was a public comment sent in response to a discussion of these themes on my feministfiguregirl.com blog site. A former sufferer from anorexia who is now a power lifter wrote:

> As a power lifter (not yet, but soon-to-be, competitive), I've found that I have begun to think about my body in terms of its proportions—NOT the "chest-hip-waist" ratio, but the "how long are my arms versus the length of my legs versus the length of my torso, and how is this going to determine my ability to efficiently complete lifts?" terms. This concern filters further out to thinking about female bodies—ANY bodies—in terms of their proportions. I look at the image of a woman and my eyes automatically scan for

a short humerus (holy benching advantage, Batman!) or a broad shoulder width, or even the direction in which their knees are naturally inclined to orient themselves throughout a walking or running stride.

In other words, I think about the image of a woman very honestly in terms of what she can likely DO before I think of the sexualized nature or lack thereof of the image before me. . . . I will tell you that as someone who formerly suffered from anorexia, the experience of strength training and now specifically power lifting has radically changed how I interpret/read the body. . . . It is possible for someone's conception of the image of the human body to change based on a significant change in the way he or she uses his or her own.[40]

This thoughtful response endorses phenomenological theories, albeit highlighting the physical capacities of human bodies rather than the instance of muscle failure. In contrast to my transformative experience, the reader arguably recalibrated her body schema by endorsing a biomechanical view of the body, viewing it as a machine made up of more or less functioning parts. I find her experience compelling because the biomedical construction of the human body is typically linked with negative effects, particularly in feminist histories of medicine. According to those accounts, from the early eighteenth century onward, the body-as-machine was objectified and medicalized, supporting physicians' claims to masterful expertise, and promoting the specialization of such fields as gynecology.[41] Calls for a return to a more holistic approach to treating the body, one that sees it as an active, unified organism, and considers emotions as part of diagnosis, are based on the rejection of biomedical models. Yet the transformed power lifter found freedom from a debilitating eating disorder by compartmentalizing her body, noting that her six-pack abs were "a sort of self-congratulation for something I've done, not the way I look."[42]

Even as weight training and working out are not in and of themselves political acts, they can have political effects. After realizing how much bodybuilding had changed me and many other women, I decided to extend that impact by linking it with feminist ethics, along the lines proposed by Simone de Beauvoir. I certified as a personal trainer with the goal of working with women in second-stage housing, offering them free access to fitness classes or one-on-one sessions. I posited that moving the body in new ways could be beneficial to formerly abused women, potentially releasing trauma that had been stored in their bodies or at least encouraging self-care. Before beginning my volunteer work, I wondered how the no doubt diverse group of women I would meet would respond to lifting heavy weights and participating in strenuous boot camp training sessions. I soon found, however, that most of the women interested in helping me—so far, I have engaged with only about ten women in second-stage housing and cannot generalize about them or my interactions with them—desired classes devoted to stretching and relaxation; they welcomed what was for many of them a rare opportunity to release tension, breathe slowly, and focus on themselves. While I am still in the process of learning about the manifold effects of exercise by pursuing this work, teaching spin classes at a local gym, and continuing with my own training, I now realize that there is no specific kind of movement, or lack of motion, that benefits all women or opens for them another world of possibilities. The experience-based perception of the body, and the dynamic nature of the body schema, mean that different forms of physicality will have different impacts on diverse women. Although such a claim might seem like common sense, it is actually at odds with any number of contemporary health and wellness movements, including those in favor as well as opposed to the current gym culture, for they all provide prescriptive solutions. Even the Health at Every Size movement promotes a natural relationship with hunger, while numerous yoga instructors encourage us to "honor the body."[43] Many feminist scholars prefer women who perform assertive, expansive motions based on the "I can" of intentionality. In the end, however, there are multiple possible ways to disrupt the body schema, should such a disruption be warranted, and they include physical instances of objectification and compartmentalization.

Conclusions

Extending the work begun in Chapter One, in this chapter I have attempted to alter conventional understandings of bodybuilding.

While weight training has typically been linked with the quest for mastery and a disciplined physique, my discussion of muscle failure instead associates it with a liberating loss of control. The instance of failure is furthermore motionless and to a certain degree senseless, at odds with feminist scholarship on the preferable forms of female embodiment. This predilection for the moving body is longstanding and can be found in a range of other sources as well as in the definition of athleticism itself. Within Western culture more broadly, athletes are identified with motion—they can run farther, jump higher, or are more agile than the rest of us—rather than with stasis. Bodybuilding features movement, both during training sessions and stage performance, but also relishes the frozen pose, when all muscles are tensed, shown to their fullest effect. Most people are aware of competitive bodybuilding primarily through the medium of still photography and thus consider the practice a motionless and feminized display sport, if they consider it a sport at all. Instead of denying the stillness involved in bodybuilding, I have offered a reevaluation of it, suggesting that immobility likewise offers opportunities for recalibrating the body schema, and undermining the standard assumption that all forms of objectification have exclusively negative consequences.

The video "Who is Heather Cassils?" was a revelation for me. In it, Cassils positions muscle failure as the basis of training; he pushes people, breaking things down before building them up again. This kind of generative destruction can also inform a feminist ethics of embodiment that would offer ways to be pushed, to have one's body schema temporarily confused, in order to open new possibilities for engaging with the world. If desired, this quest for transformation might include exercise—for I too believe that it "changes your life"—but it could be experienced by means of any number of physical experiences or situations, or by undertaking artistic activities and gestures, depending on an individual's potentially unlimited set of variables related to, among other things, gender, sexuality, ability, ethnicity, economic status, and historical experience. A feminist ethics of embodiment might even involve the concentrated effort to stay the same, refusing all change. In any case, it would never be masterful, at least not at first.

THREE

Replacing Feminism

Comparing Prochoice Activism with Becoming a Figure Girl

The two digital photographs below show the same woman. The image on the left was taken at a prochoice rally in Fredericton, New Brunswick, in 2007; the image on the right was snapped during the Northern Alberta Bodybuilding Championships in Edmonton, Alberta, in 2011. The figure in the central foreground of the left-hand picture seems serious, even angry, as she shouts into a bullhorn. Standing outside in dismal weather, in front of official-looking buildings that are in fact the provincial law courts, she is both protected and sustained by the darkly dressed woman behind her. The presence of more supporters is suggested by the truncated limbs and umbrellas that frame this snapshot-style composition. In contrast, the smiling figure on the right stands alone, on a spot-lit stage, carefully posing in a way that both recognizes the photographer and implies the presence of a larger audience. Barely clothed, she wears only an expensive, custom-made bikini and uncomfortable high-heeled shoes. Instead of legal buildings, the backdrop behind her projects another image of her body onto a large screen, reiterating the sense of display. At first glance, then, the two photographs seem to be entirely at odds, with one portraying a speaking subject engaged in socially relevant action, and the other depicting a silent object offering herself up for judgment. Some viewers might go further by characterizing the woman on the left as a feminist and,

Figure 3.1. Peggy Cooke photograph of Lianne McTavish speaking at a public prochoice demonstration in 2007, Fredericton, New Brunswick (courtesy of Peggy Cooke and Lianne McTavish).

although those involved in physique culture would immediately recognize the woman on the right as a figure competitor, others might just as easily label her an antifeminist, a postfeminist, or simply a nonfeminist.

In this chapter I want to bring these images together, creating a dialogue between them to explore issues of embodiment, politics, place, and performance. In keeping with the autoethnographic nature of previous chapters, although these photographs were taken of me, I have introduced them in the third person to undermine the presumption that they offer indexical or otherwise direct representations of me or my body.[1] The photos, I insist, signify more broadly, within a web of other images, conveying meanings that differ according to the audience regarding them. Though concerned with the vicissitudes of representing and viewing female bodies—topics addressed more fully in Chapter Five—I rarely focus my analysis on women's shifting "body image," an important albeit well-rehearsed theme, especially in relation to bodybuilding. A substantial literature

Figure 3.2. David Ford photograph of Lianne McTavish on stage at the 2011 Northern Alberta Bodybuilding Championships, Edmonton, Alberta, Tier I Figure (Medium) and Masters Figure Divisions (courtesy of Lianne McTavish).

engaging with the issue of whether bodybuilding transgresses or recuperates gender norms has firmly established that both are the case.[2] More interesting scholarship considers the various articulations of race and sexuality in bodybuilding practice, or approaches bodybuilding as a subculture.[3] In this chapter, my concerns are different. I investigate what it feels like to be a competitive figure girl, asking if the feeling is utterly distinct from being a prochoice activist. At the same time I want to compare the two practices to consider whether it is possible to embody feminism and, if so, what that would feel like.

This emphasis on thinking through lived experience extends the discussion of phenomenological theory begun in the previous chapter, highlighting the intersubjectivity of the body, which according to Maurice Merleau-Ponty perceives a world filled with opportunities for action, and cannot be separated from it. In the discussion below, I attend to bodies in two different worlds, using as case studies my volunteer work as a prochoice escort in Fredericton, guiding women and their families into the Morgentaler Abortion Clinic between 1999 and 2007, and my subsequent entry into the world of bodybuilding in Edmonton, from 2008 until the present day. I once assumed that my physical activities in Edmonton constituted a break from my political work in Fredericton. I came to question that idea, however, after reading some of the growing scholarship on the production of "place." Such feminist geographers as Heidi J. Nast and Steve Pile study "the ways in which bodies and places are understood, how they are made and how they are interrelated, one to the other—because this is how we live our lives—through places, through the body."[4] Along with other researchers, Nast and Pile investigate how spaces become meaningful places that contribute to the production of subjectivity, are embedded in power relations, and are renegotiated.[5] By drawing my attention to the constant interaction of bodies and places, this literature led me to find surprising similarities between my prochoice activism in the streets of Fredericton and my bodybuilding at the gym in Edmonton. As I will argue below, both activities involved the pleasures and perils of performing within an overtly theatrical public space, relied on the reiteration of gendered identities, and produced concomitant forms of embodied authority, for myself as well as for the others necessarily included in this discussion.[6]

My decision to compare prochoice lobbying with bodybuilding also stems from the most common question I received about my ongoing research project: "What is feminist about Feminist Figure Girl?" This query, never posed in relation to my prochoice work, was typically raised about my bodybuilding project in a skeptical or challenging manner by self-identified feminists of various stripes. At the beginning of the project I admitted my uncertainty in regard to this question, as well as my openness to the potentially antifeminist aspects of dieting, squeezing into a tiny bikini, and learning to walk in high heels. I gradually realized, however, that by entering a figure competition I had not abandoned my ethical commitments to or participation in feminist communities; I had both interrogated and expanded on them. Instead of the standard "before and after" narrative implied by the photographs juxtaposed above—a narrative exploited in several newspaper reports about Feminist Figure Girl, which noted my transformation from frumpy professor to glamour girl—I found a feminist continuum.[7] This chapter thus intervenes in debates about how feminism is currently being transformed. The elusive terms "postfeminism" and "third-wave feminism" are sometimes similarly defined as recent movements that reject the second-wave feminism of the 1970s that was devoted to, among other things, the pursuit of sisterhood and reproductive rights, to embrace more individualistic and superficial explorations of a range of gendered identities.[8] Although I seriously consider this negative assessment, in the end I endorse more positive understandings of recent forms of feminism as sites of risk that expand beyond a feminist audience to admit multiple subject positions.[9] For me, becoming a figure girl was a site of minimal risk, one largely determined by the places I inhabited physically and by the people inhabiting them with me. It was a risk worth taking, for I did not replace feminist politics with something less important; I "re-placed" feminism by moving to another location, responding to a different situation that opened new experiences and possibilities, without constituting a radical rejection of the past.

Embodying Prochoice Work in Fredericton

To my knowledge, nothing substantial has been written about the embodied experiences of prochoice activists or clinic escorts. In

contrast, scholarly considerations of the fleshly experience of pregnancy, childbirth, miscarriage, and abortion have been produced by,
among others, historians, feminists, and anthropologists.[10] Narratives devoted to feminist activism have instead focused on its social
circumstances and political results.[11] The physical experience of
being "on the front lines" of struggles over reproductive rights is
nevertheless both intense and memorable. I first volunteered as a
clinic escort at the Planned Parenthood of Rochester and the Gen-
esee Valley during the early 1990s, when I was a graduate student
at the University of Rochester in New York. With other prochoice
feminists, I patrolled the sidewalks outside the clinic during the
run-up to the 1992 Presidential election, when Democratic nomi-
nee Bill Clinton eventually displaced the incumbent George H.W.
Bush, a conservative Republican. These Saturday mornings typically
involved physical confrontations with "enemy" antiabortion protestors, who intercepted women coming to the clinic (for prenatal testing, birth control information, or abortion services) and restrained
volunteers. This stressful situation was exacerbated when the radical antiabortion group Operation Rescue attempted to blockade
clinics in nearby Buffalo during the spring of 1992.[12] I linked arms
with hundreds of others to form human chains around the entrances
to these clinics, chanting prochoice and anticonservative slogans
while being scrutinized by media, police officers, and members of
the American Civil Liberties Union. My tired and often dehydrated
body was tensed, ready to respond to protestors charging the lines,
or to instructions from those directing prochoice strategy. At the
same time, my body was literally supported by those of other like-
minded volunteers as we formed a protective network. Overall, the
experience was empowering, creating a sense of feminist community,
but as a Canadian student I remained an outsider, presumably more
vulnerable to being arrested than to being denied a legal abortion.

When I returned to Canada to begin work as a professor at the
University of New Brunswick, I became immersed in a rather different situation, co-creating and then supervising the volunteer escorts
at the Morgentaler abortion clinic. The small city of Fredericton—
in 2006 its population was just over 50,000—is located along the
banks of the Saint John River in New Brunswick, one of three Mari-
time Provinces on the east coast of Canada. As the provincial capital,
Fredericton hosts two universities and contains a mixture of social

conservatives and liberals, as well as a sizeable francophone population comprised mainly of Acadians. When the abortion rights crusader Dr. Henry Morgentaler first opened a clinic in Fredericton in 1994, the conservative elements of the city responded negatively, calling for the clinic to be banned.[13] Despite being unable to prevent the clinic from operating, the government of New Brunswick has consistently refused to fund the abortions performed there. Provincial governments are responsible for the administration and delivery of health care services, having some leeway in such decisions as where to locate hospitals and how much money to expend. The provinces must, however, adhere to the *Canada Health Act*, passed in 1984, to receive transfer payments from the federal government.[14] This *Act* includes principles designed to ensure that Canadian citizens have equal access to medically necessary services administered publicly on a nonprofit basis. All provinces have recognized abortion as a medically required service, but the government of New Brunswick has created policies that limit access to it.[15] Canadians thus pursue and receive reproductive health care in diverse ways that are influenced by a range of factors, including geographical location.

In order to qualify for a funded hospital abortion in New Brunswick, women must obtain the written approval of one physician and one gynecologist. Known as Regulation 84-20, this policy is both unique to New Brunswick and at odds with the Supreme Court ruling of 1988, which struck down Canada's abortion regulations as discriminatory, arguing that they violated the Charter of Rights and Freedoms as well as the principles of fundamental justice. In contrast to Alberta, where abortion is funded in clinics up to twenty weeks of gestation, in New Brunswick women must make haste to receive the two approvals because the provincial government limits coverage to the termination of pregnancies under twelve weeks of gestation.[16] Since 2006, only two hospitals in New Brunswick have provided these abortion services, performing about twenty procedures per month, though I have heard through the grapevine that one hospital will soon cease to offer the procedure because of staffing and budgetary limitations. Given these unique regulations, New Brunswick women are routinely denied hospital abortions, especially in the predominantly Roman Catholic Saint John region. Every year around 800 women pay out-of-pocket for abortions obtained at the Morgentaler Clinic in Fredericton.[17]

This situation has encouraged antiabortion protestors to picket near the clinic when it is open on Tuesdays, carrying signs plastered with slogans and enlarged images of embryos or fetuses. They regularly attempt to intercept women who are entering the clinic, misdirecting them into the antiabortion "Pregnancy Care Centre" next door to the abortion clinic.[18] Most clients live in New Brunswick and are driving from diverse parts of the province, particularly the Saint John region. A small number travel from Prince Edward Island, deciding to pay for the procedure in Fredericton because it requires a single visit instead of multiple hospital appointments in Halifax. As the supervisor of other escorts, I scheduled three shifts of two pairs of volunteers for every Tuesday morning. The volunteer corps consisted of men and women of all ages but included many university students, especially law students committed to pursuing social justice. On clinic days, we would check in at the front desk and then perform such mundane tasks as snow shoveling until the patients started arriving. At that point our attention shifted to helping women and their families enter the clinic. In contrast to the lively and unstable conditions that I had encountered while volunteering in the United States, in Canada the situation was predictable and even monotonous. The boredom was disrupted in an unpleasant manner when protestors charged toward and shouted at potential patients. All the same, the work was rewarding, for we received praise from every person who entered the clinic, motivating us to continue acting as volunteers week in and week out, year after year.

A passage from my journal at the time captures a typical interaction near the entrance of the clinic:

> I breathe shallowly through the silver pashmina shawl wrapped around my upper face and neck, overtop of the fleece warmer from Mountain Equipment Coop. The freezing cold is thick and oppressive, targeting my vulnerable feet and creeping up through my body. The foot-warming pouches that I awkwardly placed inside my boots have yet to start working. Even so, I remain alert, scanning the sidewalks for movement, watching to see if passing cars slow down. I notice two women approaching the clinic from about a block away. I am not the only one who sees them. A middle-aged gangly protestor with long blonde hair—we call her

"Crazy Legs" because she often wears patterned slacks while chasing our patients—tosses her sign into the snow and sets off toward them in a determined fashion. Without speaking, my fellow escort and I immediately depart, aiming to reach the women first. My fit, strong body easily overtakes that of Crazy Legs, now huffing with exertion. She looks desperate and starts to scream, "Don't kill your baby. They are liars!" Resolutely ignoring her, I smile and calmly introduce myself to the two strangers, adding, "You have quite a welcoming committee today. You might like to turn up that iPod as we enter the clinic, the yellow brick building on the right." I politely hold the door open and the women say thanks. Once they are inside, I laugh out loud. Squashing the anger that bubbles inside me, I wait for my heart rate to decrease.

When I walked with patients, physically shielding their bodies from protestors with my own, I often initiated a conversation about the weather, a form of social ritual designed to normalize an otherwise unpleasant situation. We would discuss the cold and potential for snow storms while being screamed at and swarmed by antiabortion protestors. According to cultural theorist Jody Berland, conversations about the weather are far from neutral. Canadians continually comment on the temperature to create both a shared sense of identity and what she calls "the pleasure of the located body."[19] Berland argues that discourses about the weather attempt both to control and deny its significance, and are central to regional identities. My conversations about the climate in New Brunswick were indeed ambivalent: I attempted to bond with those entering the clinic by joking about the highways they had just driven, particularly the treacherous Route 7 that stretches between Saint John and Fredericton and is typically covered in ice as well as moose during the winter months. We employ narratives about the weather to create what historian Carroll Smith-Rosenberg calls the fantasy of a coherent body politic, achieving "a sense of homogeneity in an otherwise diverse populace."[20] This communication held particular significance outside the clinic, for it established an immediate sense of community between escorts and abortion-seeking women—groups that in reality might have had little in common.

In front of the Morgentaler Clinic, we confirmed our status as vigorous and good-humored Maritimers able to overcome the natural elements. This temporary and in many ways fictional identity—I am originally from Ontario—allowed me and other escorts to show concern for the well-being of incoming women, signaling respect for their decision to have an abortion without invading their privacy. This commentary on the weather reinforced a commonplace image of embodiment, but it also led to discussions of particular bodies. Without any prompting on my part, the women coming to the clinic regularly remarked on their physical exhaustion after getting up at 5:00 a.m. to drive from the north shore, or on their bladders, which were uncomfortably full in preparation for the ultrasounds to be performed inside the clinic. When they requested permission to relieve this pressure, staff inside the clinic would suggest that the women half-empty their bladders, a physical challenge most had not previously contemplated.

I also spoke with the women who periodically came outside to smoke cigarettes. I interpreted this activity as both the women's desire for nicotine and their defiant insistence on bodily pleasure in the face of the protestors. Some women felt vulnerable outside the clinic, wondering if they would be physically attacked by the protestors. Other women were adamantly certain of their right to have an abortion and shouted right back at the protestors while shivering in the smoking area. Many of these women explained their reasons for having an abortion, telling me that at sixteen years old they were too young to have a child, that their pre-existing medical conditions would be exacerbated by a pregnancy, that they had been raped, or that they already had more children than they could support. Whether part of a deliberate strategy or not, these statements and physical demonstrations worked to counteract the abstract understanding of the female body promoted by the protestors.[21]

Much literature on the production of place focuses on the locations and practices of human dwelling, but the space around the Morgentaler Clinic, a one-story yellow-brick edifice in the modernist style, was usually empty. On Tuesday mornings people inhabited it temporarily, standing outside to smoke, chat, or work as escorts. Others merely passed through it on their way to some other place. In the absence of protestors and escorts, the perimeter around the clinic is unremarkable, consisting of sidewalks, paved streets, and a nondescript parking garage. To a certain extent the building itself is responsible for demarcating the significance of place, and yet the clinic exists because of governmental policies that segregate abortion from the regular provision of health care. When abortions are integrated into hospital settings, they attract little attention from protestors, who are unable to distinguish abortion-seeking women from those seeking other kinds of health care, or unwilling to display themselves before a wide public. It is nevertheless most accurate to say that the building becomes visible only when protestors and escorts are present because their interactions draw people's attention to the clinic, often for the first time. Members of the public have remarked that they had not even noticed the building before seeing the protestors. The activities occurring outside the clinic on Tuesday mornings also contributed to the meaning of the interior of the building. The presence of protestors encouraged many abortion-seeking women to rush toward the clinic and breathe a sigh of relief once inside. Though the protestors tried to demonize the clinic, they actually transformed it into a kind of refuge for women.

Protestors and escorts alike attempted to manage how the space near the clinic became significant, controlling how it would be experienced by the women who traversed it to enter the building, as well as by those people simply passing through or driving by. The temporary place created around the clinic on Tuesday mornings effectively became a forum for the theatrical performance of political identities. Escorts wore costumes, consisting of blue aprons emblazoned with the words "Clinic Escort." Incoming clients had been advised by clinic staff to look for patrolling escorts as their helpers, a role that made me feel powerful, even heroic. Other escorts had similar reactions—one young volunteer even wore a spandex superhero costume during her shift. Her playful performance made light of the confrontational situation at the clinic while amusing the women who were arriving for their appointments. During the summer of 2007, an unknown young man arrived with a mock light-saber in hand, ready to "battle" the antiabortion demonstrators. Recognizing the theatricality of the space outside the clinic, he played the role of a Jedi warrior fighting for justice. At the same time, his actions revealed as performative the identities of everyone occupying the same space, including mine.

The prochoice uniform also created a sense of group identity among escorts, something that was more overtly promoted during the training sessions that I regularly provided. Whenever a new volunteer arrived, I would have them don an apron and then watch me work, all the while offering advice about the bodily comportment expected of them. They were to move deliberately and confidently, never running toward potential patients. I would encourage them to be convivial, keeping the conversation light and refusing to engage with the protestors. "We are here for the women, not for them," I would declare. "Those opposed to legal abortion need us to constitute their identities, but we do not need them for anything." I had indeed found that the protestors loathed being ignored as well as seeing us laugh together or joke with patients. Although I tried not to be dictatorial, I did not like it when volunteers refused to play this role. If they smoked or sat down on the job, I would move them to less visible positions behind the clinic. The performance of prochoice identity furthermore required that negative or strong emotions be controlled at all times. Escorts were instructed to remain calm, never acknowledging the taunts and catcalls of the protestors, never expressing extreme sorrow at the troublesome stories sometimes related by women accessing the clinic. When one new recruit insisted on hugging all clients to show her support, and occasionally shedding a tear, I stopped scheduling her for shifts. Overall, then, prochoice escorts were fashioned as neatly attired, reasonable, fun-loving, and caring people who mostly minded their own business.

The main quality required of a clinic escort at the Morgentaler clinic in Fredericton was endurance. We tolerated the seemingly relentless efforts of the protestors, who never once succeeded in "talking" a woman out of her decision to have an abortion. Even more so, we carried on despite the physical demands of the job, primarily those related to changeable climactic conditions. Standing outside in the freezing cold made me acutely aware of my body and its limitations. When temperatures dropped well below freezing, I would schedule an extra volunteer so we could take turns going inside the clinic to warm up and take deep rather than shallow breaths. For me at least, the complicated interaction between diverse bodies in a specific space for measured periods of time created a particular form of prochoice embodied experience. My political body was based on the principles of control and fortitude and the display of learned behaviors, embodied knowledge that I conveyed to other volunteers. Displaying this managed body gave me a sense of authority and self-satisfaction. It also provided me with respectable feminist credentials that I revealed when lobbying government officials, using a megaphone to argue for reproductive justice at public protests, or exchanging stories at women's studies conferences. Unfortunately, my prochoice volunteer work diminished when I relocated to western Canada.

Building Bodies in Edmonton

As soon as I arrived in Edmonton to begin my position at the University of Alberta, I contacted the local Morgentaler Clinic, called Women's Health Options, to offer my services. I learned, however, that escorts were not required. After the Edmonton clinic was attacked with toxic butyric acid in 1996, an injunction was put in place to prohibit protesting within a fixed distance of the building.[22] I therefore turned my prochoice attentions to a so-called Crisis Pregnancy Centre in town which, like other organizations of this kind, was run by an antiabortion group that claimed to offer neutral counseling about pregnancy options, and then bombarded unsuspecting women with propaganda, misinforming them that abortion would increase their risk of developing breast cancer and future miscarriage. Among other activities, I would rise early in the mornings to poster my neighborhood with signs stating simply that those at the centre were opposed to legal abortion. These political interventions were rewarding, but I eventually stopped them because the time commitment and flexibility required were interfering with my publishing schedule. While continuing to advocate for the principles of reproductive justice as a Board Member and spokesperson for ARCC, the Abortion Rights Coalition of Canada, I instead wrote about my earlier experiences as a prochoice activist in both the United States and Canada, bringing my volunteer and academic work together in an overt manner.[23] Around the same time, I commenced lifting heavy weights at the gym.

My attraction to weight lifting was site specific, for Alberta is a hotbed of bodybuilding within Canada. So far, my efforts to understand this phenomenon have been unsuccessful. When I asked my

first personal trainer, competitive heavyweight bodybuilder Gillian
Kovack, why bodybuilding was so popular in Edmonton—this pros-
perous northern city of over a million inhabitants is dependent on
the boom-and-bust oil economy—she jokingly responded, "Well, I
guess there is nothing else to do here."[24] Equally unconvincing were
others' suggestions that the long, dark winters in Edmonton had
forced angry people indoors to expend their energies by picking up
heavy things. In any case, an appreciation of physique culture is evident in the urban centers of Alberta, as it is in some American cities
and other parts of the world. My rationalization for why this appreciation flourishes in Edmonton rather than, say, Saskatoon, is that a
dedicated handful of people living here built their bodies and established organizations devoted to promoting bodybuilding, including
the Alberta Bodybuilding Association.[25] The high visibility of practitioners and competitions within the city encourages people to participate in physique culture or at least to recognize its value, making
it more likely for them to have a family member or friend involved
in bodybuilding contests.

All the same, my interest in bodybuilding was neither happen-
stance nor unrelated to my research. As a specialist in seventeenth-
century European visual culture, medicine, and the body, I had
offered introductory undergraduate courses on The History of the
Body, spanning from the medieval through the contemporary periods. Images of contemporary bodybuilding, in popular magazines
as well as in the film *Pumping Iron* (1977), were analyzed in my
classrooms during discussions of gender and sexuality. Once I could
afford to hire a personal trainer, I deliberately selected Gill, the most
muscular woman I had ever seen outside of the film *Pumping Iron
II: The Women* (1985).[26] I admired both her commitment to fitness
and her willingness to eschew standard definitions of femininity. As
a large woman able to bench press far more than the average man,
Gill was subject to intense scrutiny while at the gym, not to mention the lascivious reactions and occasional ridicule she encountered
when outside of it. After I began to lift (what were for me) heavy
weights with her while following her nutrition advice, we became
close friends. I slowly entered the world of competitive bodybuilding, first as her assistant tan applier and towel fetcher, and then by
taking to the stage myself. During the next four years, bodybuilding

provided me with a community that replaced the prochoice relationships I had left behind and was sorely missing.

This community took shape within a specific place, namely a large, commercial gym located on the ground floor of a high-rise building in downtown Edmonton. I continue to train there six days a week. Following a standardized design, the first floor of this gym features a reception area as well as rows of modern cardio equipment—stationary bicycles, elliptical machines, and step mills—with personalized television screens. The brightly lighted basement houses the locker rooms as well as fifty weight-lifting machines, multiple squat racks, and a large free-weight area. This space, with its gray concrete floor, mirrored walls, and bright corporate colors, was where I spent, and still spend, most of my time at the gym. I generally avoid the sequestered "women's only" training room at the back, for it contains only a few benches, mats, and lighter dumbbells. Instead, I use free weights and smith machines while in the mixed space, training with paid female professionals, female friends, or on my own.

A substantial scholarly literature explores the communities built in relation to organized fitness activities, noting that different kinds of gyms—for instance those devoted to boxing or located in suburban areas—will foster distinctive cultures.[27] New gyms are continually created to support specific demographics in today's consumer culture. A chain called Downsize Fitness that recently opened in three American cities caters exclusively to clients with fifty or more pounds to lose.[28] "Skinny" people are not allowed to join. In the past, gyms committed to making clients feel comfortable have excluded male members. The North American chain Curves advertises "no men, no mirrors," reassuring those female patrons who fear being looked at and judged.[29] This franchise also prefers to hire "average" support staff, not educated trainers with visible musculature. Such specialized organizations reveal that certain groups, especially overweight or unfit women, have had negative experiences with exercise, realizing that gyms primarily function as sites of display rather than mutual support. The spatial dynamics of gyms can indeed have a profound impact on self-perception. In keeping with my previous discussion of how the space surrounding the Morgentaler clinic in Fredericton reshapes the identities of those who enter it, I have observed that exercisers who are of average size while at a theater, shopping mall, or restaurant are suddenly transformed into fat people when they enter a standard commercial gym. Surrounded by motivational posters, scales, and heart rate charts, as well as by a number of athletes, they can be seen and see themselves differently, becoming both disoriented and understandably resentful. As the active field of fat studies is revealing, the categories of fat and fit are historically and culturally determined; they are also dependent on the vagaries of place.[30]

My experiences of bodybuilding culture reveal that it too occurs within specific places that create distinctions. Working out, lifting weights, or even having visible musculature does not make someone a bodybuilder. When I first started exercising regularly in graduate school, I favored stress-relieving aerobics, a practice that I continued after moving to Fredericton. There I also lifted weights in choreographed group exercise classes, and became stronger, but I was by no means a bodybuilder. Bodybuilding requires focused training that isolates distinctive muscles and muscle groups, growing them with an emphasis on balance and symmetry, not simply size, to create an ideal form: roughly speaking, a wide upper body tapers to a narrow waist and then flares out again with substantial buttocks and legs. Bodybuilding furthermore requires a careful consideration of diet, typically one much higher in protein and lower in carbohydrates and saturated fats than that of the average person. Before residing in Edmonton, I was not eating "clean" in this fashion and therefore had a significant amount of body fat, despite working out five days per week. A real bodybuilder trains in a goal-oriented and methodical way—rarely lifting as heavy as possible—while measuring the results both numerically and visually. He or she eventually exhibits the resulting physique on stage during a competition, an identity-affirming ritual described in the next chapter. In contrast, athletes and other exercisers lift weights for manifold reasons: to gain strength in order to skate faster, to reach a new personal best in power-lifting contests, or to hit a golf ball farther. Though these people might display impressive physiques at the gym and draw on bodybuilding techniques to shape their training programs, they are not bodybuilders.

My definition of bodybuilding is based on first-hand observations made at the gym, especially while preparing for a figure contest held in June 2011. I was arguably a bodybuilder only during a brief period between 2010 and 2011, the year I spent training specifically for my competition. My identity in relation to the gym has in fact always been in flux. In keeping with my experiences of prochoice volunteer work, I began bodybuilding as a novice, receiving instruction from experts and by means of embodied experience, and then moved up through the ranks to a teaching position. Whereas in New Brunswick I had become a prochoice lobbyist and clinic escort supervisor, in Edmonton I certified as a personal trainer and now lead spin classes at my gym. My transformation at the gym occurred within various spaces, which shaped my body even as I inhabited and became visible within them. When I was a newbie to fitness culture, I performed choreographed aerobic movements under the direction of a group fitness instructor. Sweating within a large studio space outfitted with full-length mirrors, I felt my experience as one of shared physicality and sociability, a phenomenon analyzed in sophisticated studies by media scholars and specialists in cultural studies.[31] Once I started training like a bodybuilder, I left that space, never to return.

> After completing six sets of fifteen lying leg curls at 90 pounds, and four sets of fifteen leg presses at 320 pounds, my trainer and I moved on to the hack squat machine. I crouched down, "ass to ankles," with 120 pounds on my shoulders. Rising to a standing position took all of my concentration, all of my effort. Without deliberating, I pushed. A warm, intense energy suffused my stressed glutes and hams, and then spread throughout my body. Between sets, I dizzily exited the machine, feeling a wave of delicious nausea. No. It was more like an unsettling hallucination. My body was engulfed; I was overwhelmed; I no longer existed.

In many ways this shift of location marked a decline in my status. Arguably one of the fittest members of my group step, kickboxing, and aerobics classes, I was weak and ignorant within the weight-lifting areas of the gym. My slow and steady education took place over two years, providing me with novel physical experiences and a body that navigated space and time differently. From my trainers I learned how to isolate specific muscles, flexing some while deliberately disengaging others. I would, for instance, contract my quadriceps during sissy squats, rising from a crouched position without throwing my back into the movement or using momentum. I would lower a heavy barbell to the floor while performing a straight-legged dead lift, and then primarily deploy my hamstring muscles to return to a standing position. I practiced taking a deep breath, adopting a set position, and then mechanically pushing or lifting weights while breathing out to get a better "pump" during each motion. Because every movement was measured and timed, I found myself counting almost continually, two down and two up for a biceps curl, while keeping track of five sets of eight to ten repetitions, and looking at the clock to take a one-minute rest between each set. My weekly schedule, already filled with writing deadlines, teaching, and meetings, was altered to accommodate a split training program. I worked back on Mondays, chest on Tuesdays, legs on Wednesdays, arms on Thursdays, legs again on Fridays, and shoulders on Saturdays. I started to organize my career and social life around my workouts, finding a surprising degree of fulfillment in my gradually increasing strength and ability.

My body was expanding in other ways, as I was more aware of it, both in and out of the gym. My trainer used multisensory methods to teach me how to move and perceive my body. When instructing me in a new exercise, she would demonstrate the technique and provide verbal advice while guiding me through my first attempt, touching the major muscles engaged to draw my full attention to them. It became clear to me that working out required intellectual effort to produce muscle memory, so that, as she said, "my body could figure out what I was telling it to do."[32] This memory results from the repetition of movement as well as an increase in brain activity, which decreases once the motor skill has been learned. I started to locate intelligence throughout my body, noticing other kinds of physical skills that I had previously acquired and then forgotten. I became newly aware of which muscles I was using during the mundane activities of my everyday life, striving to make them more efficient while avoiding strain or imbalances. At the same time, my body was often sore in the areas targeted during training sessions, experiencing DOMS (delayed onset muscle soreness), which caused me to move stiffly up the stairs on campus and take opportunities to stretch while standing in line to buy coffee. In short, my body was omnipresent in a way it had never been before.

After swinging my feet underneath the apparatus, I lightly press my legs forward, ensuring that the flat black pad will be safely lifted by my strong shins rather than my more vulnerable knees or weak ankles. I lean back, arranging myself on the vinyl chair so that I look good: tummy flat and triceps delineated. Turning away from the mirror, I reach down to move the pin into the 160-pound weight block, hoping that someone at the gym will notice and be impressed. After a few preparatory breaths, I thrust both legs upward, straightening my knees while trying to relax my upper body so that the stress is borne exclusively by my quadriceps. The movement is mechanical, as if a doctor is using a hammer to check my reflexes. This kicking is, however, purposeful and controlled. At the top of each swing, I flex my feet and intensify the contraction in my muscles, feeling an extra pulse of pressure directly above each knee, before slowly lowering my legs back down again. When the burning becomes too intense, I move the pin to decrease the weight by ten pounds, and immediately restart my repetitions. Visualizing numbers in my head, I count toward fifty, as if in a *"Sesame Street"* lesson. Clenching my teeth, and grunting with exertion, my eyes become unfocused. Everything goes blank, and I am alone.

My embodied regime eventually allowed me to identify with certain members of the fitness community while distinguishing myself from others. I was comfortable at the gym, knowing how to recognize, adjust, and use every apparatus in the weight-training area. I came to understand the underlying logic of modern gyms, and can now negotiate an unknown one, just as a seasoned traveler easily navigates any airport in the world. I had in effect learned what sociologist Pierre Bourdieu calls the "rules of the game," which are created when social actors develop a certain disposition for action, including a set of typical body movements and mannerisms, within specific fields or settings.[33] At the gym these movements extend beyond knowing how to lift weights properly to include numerous rules of etiquette. I realized, for instance, that I should not stand directly in front of a person lifting weights, thereby blocking access to the mirror. Nor should I neglect to rerack dumbbells, refuse to share equipment (i.e., let someone "work in"), drop barbells to the floor with a thud, or walk away from a sweaty bench without wiping it down. Exercisers without an understanding of equipment, spatial dynamics, and the conventions of bodily comportment, such as beginners and many women, are not excluded from the weight-training areas of the gym per se, but they are likely to feel ill at ease among bodybuilders.

Once I started dieting for my competition, my muscularity became visible and I was more easily identified as a bodybuilder, not just a fitness enthusiast. Even for an entry-level contest such as the one in which I participated, most competitors have spent years building muscle, working out methodically while eating high-protein foods. They have then "dieted down," losing fat (and inevitably some muscle mass) in order to become lean and make that musculature evident. This period usually lasts between three and five months, and includes an increased and measured intake of selected supplements as well as regular posing and tanning sessions. I began my precompetition diet in January of 2011, starting with a body that weighed 142 pounds and contained 16 percent fat. When I took to the stage on June 4 of that year, I was 118 pounds and had about 6 percent body fat. Yet even three months before the competition I was becoming noticeably "ripped," and was regularly approached by people at the gym as well as on the street or in the grocery store, asking me when I would be on stage. My muscular body became more public and open to commentary. One evening in May, I entered a bodybuilding store to buy more supplies—including a rather disgusting zero-calorie, zero-carbohydrate, sugar-free brand of pancake syrup as a "treat"—and found another competitor behind the counter. Barely awake, he managed to ring in my items slowly as we traded diet stories. His rigid diet coach had already removed artificial sweeteners, sugar-free gum, and sodium from his regime, whereas mine had ordered me to eat more chicken and protein pancakes (made of egg whites and protein powder blended and cooked without oil). We both admitted to avoiding stairs, falling asleep at work, and craving peanut butter. The instant bond between us was based on our shared embodied experience but also on our current state of vulnerability. Preparing to compete in a bodybuilding show means inviting weakness and potential failure as much as it involves taking pride in the discipline involved and body produced. Competing is a risky venture, and most people who start the process never reach their goal of being "stage ready," finding it both physically and psychologically impossible.

Visibility and display are the key aspects emphasized in most scholarly accounts of bodybuilding, but they were not the most important ones for me.[34] During my competition preparation I was simply exhausted. As a person usually brimming with energy, able to be productive from morning until night, feeling tired was a shocking revelation. For the first time in my life I needed to sit down and do nothing at several points throughout the day. During the last few months before the show, I had to stop attending spin classes, restricting my daily one-hour cardio sessions to the step mill—a kind of never-ending escalator—set only at level five or six. Practically a zombie, I nevertheless lifted weights every day, following the program created by my personal trainer and the advice of my diet coach to the letter. I think the discipline and organizational skills required during this precompetition period were not as challenging for me as they were (and are) for others. I had already experienced what it felt like to work steadily and repetitively toward a distant goal, both by pursuing a doctoral degree and volunteering as a pro-choice escort.

All the same, my self-perception changed in significant ways during the run-up to my competition, arguably not for the better. I was already accustomed to observing myself in mirrors, checking my form while working out, but for five months my body was increasingly objectified. Every Friday I was weighed, measured, and then photographed while wearing a string bikini—the first one I had ever owned—to provide information for my diet coach. In addition to scrutinizing these pictures, I constantly looked for signs of muscle mass in mirrors at the gym, at home, or while walking through the mall. After paying relatively little attention to my appearance for the first forty-two years of my life, I became obsessed with how I looked, spending exorbitant amounts of money on laser hair removal sessions, microdermabrasion facials, teeth-whitening strips, and salon treatments designed to make my long dark hair both blonde and silky. I kept telling myself that conforming vigorously to the conventional norms of feminine beauty was a key part of my research project. In reality, I had become more invested in how I looked; I cared about the reactions of others, especially straight men, to my new image. On one hand, I analyzed this transformation (and discuss its economic implications in Chapter Four), realizing that while I was technically not more attractive than before, I was rewarded for my concerted efforts to comply with the social standards of beauty by wearing makeup and pursuing a slender frame. On the other hand, I reveled in my newfound hotness, displaying my small waist and perky breasts in tight jeans and tank tops, flirting with men and women alike in bars and cafes.

This experience of gender conformity was in many ways the most confusing and illuminating aspect of the Feminist Figure Girl project. It was also the most controversial, inciting questions from feminist as well as other critics.[35] Women have long been identified with appearance and evaluated more on their attractiveness than on such contributions as textile making, childbearing, novel writing, and crop planting. Feminist scholarship has often drawn attention to the intellectual and political accomplishments of women in the past, correcting the longstanding emphasis on female beauty. While writing my doctoral thesis in Paris in 1994, I had, for instance, undertaken archival work on the little-known female members of the Royal Academy of Painting and Sculpture during the seventeenth century.[36] Yet in my Feminist Figure Girl research I was almost snubbing my nose at my professional training, refusing to do what was expected of me by celebrating superficial qualities. This aspect of the project, along with my eventual onstage comparison with other women in what was in effect a beauty contest, troubled me throughout the process.

In many ways, physique culture creates divisions among women, and not just those deemed fit or fat. Bodybuilding organizations support various competitive categories for female contestants, including figure, fitness, bikini, and different levels of bodybuilding. Figure was introduced as an official category by the National Physique Committee in 2001 to offset the increasing size and musculature of female heavyweight bodybuilders, which some viewers found too extreme and "masculine," as discussed earlier.[37] The heavyweight look was furthermore difficult to market within the fitness industry. Figure requires women to achieve a less muscular body than that of traditional bodybuilders and to focus on overall shape as well as "feminine" aesthetic appeal. Yet when many figure girls defiantly began to adopt a harder, more muscular look that moved them closer to the category of traditional bodybuilding, an additional competitive category was created: bikini. As previously mentioned, these contests, arguably now the most popular kind, feature soft, thin, pretty women with large breast implants. Instead of displaying musculature or the results of athletic training, "bikini girls" must skip across the stage and push their breasts out toward the audience, before turning around to arch their backs while thrusting out their buttocks. According to my observations, both at the gym and during competitions, bikini girls are not (yet) respected within the fitness industry, and certainly not by serious bodybuilders.[38] I suspect that at least some bikini girls will also gradually become more muscular in appearance, striving to display their labor visibly, before yet another competitive category is added, or more rigid "femininity" rules are introduced by official bodybuilding organizations.

Despite recognizing and participating in this divisiveness, I found that becoming a figure girl also reinforced and extended many of the feminist principles I had learned in graduate school and as a prochoice escort. My new identity helped me to find and create a female community in Edmonton. Many men encouraged me, but my main source of support came from female fitness enthusiasts, especially Audrey Shepherd, the personal trainer I hired when Gill retired to become a professional bodybuilder full time. After designing my program, which changed every six weeks and included a thrilling power-lifting segment right before I began my diet, Audrey worked out with me twice a week. She also took pictures of me every month, helped me learn how to walk in high heels, and took video of these sessions for later analysis. Other figure girls, especially Deanna Harder, a well-educated trainer who had competed four times, took a personal interest in my progress, providing advice and posing tips. These sessions often involved laughter when I consistently failed to comply with the gendered motions associated with walking like a sexy woman.

Given my clear lack of talent, I began taking weekly lessons in how to move like a figure girl from professional coach and former figure champion Raejha Douziech. My no-nonsense posing instructor would frequently tell me to pull up my shoulders while sticking out my chest and butt. No matter how hard I tried, my body would not comply; I could never "work it" by walking in a way that was gracefully sexy yet tinged with an air of innocent confidence, remember the proper hand positions, or position my feet just so. On the day of the competition I placed tenth out of the twenty-three competitors on stage, downgraded because of my lack of presentation skills. I was not the only aspiring figure girl who found posing to be the most difficult part of the process; many other contestants struggled with it, admitting they were more like athletic tomboys than beauty queens. Our group practice sessions often involved deliberately exaggerated movements, as we strove to achieve the ideal feminine form by pretending to be drag queens.

This heightened experience of "femininity as a masquerade" encouraged me to reevaluate the work of Judith Butler. I had read *Gender Trouble* in graduate school, benefitting from the requisite training in psychoanalysis from Kaja Silverman, but was always wary of the seemingly shorthand or flippant way in which Butler's arguments about the performance of gender could be invoked, as if they were self-evident.[39] Her insistence that gender was not a stable identity but a mundane combination of bodily gestures and movements to create the illusion of an abiding gendered self was perfectly acceptable to me before my figure training;[40] during my competition preparation I literally lived it. Bodybuilding and figure competitions are essentially stylized repetitions of acts through time, though these acts are performed in a seemingly deliberate way, even as Butler's claim that "the body is not passively scripted with cultural codes . . . [b]ut neither do embodied selves pre-exist the cultural conventions which essentially signify bodies" was made manifest.[41] The competition script pre-existed me, and though I attempted to conform to its limitations, I unwittingly enacted it differently. This ritual taught me that I would never become a figure girl, would never reach that ideal, and no other woman would either. My failure was not a disappointment so much as an intensely revealing experience, teaching me far more about gender than my prochoice activism had done.

Questions about my Feminist Figure Girl project nevertheless remained. Did it signal a move away from my earlier prochoice work—easily classified as a "second wave" feminist activity—to something different, potentially labeled "third-wave" feminism or even "postfeminism?" During the 1990s, the term "third wave" invoked a deliberate rejection of many of the feminist practices promoted during the 1960s and 1970s, a move toward new strategies informed by a commitment to cultural and racial diversity, sex positivity, and micropolitics.[42] Even as feminists recognized the contentious nature of the classification, they adopted the name "third wave" to distinguish themselves from the perceived dominance of middle-class, white women in second-wave feminism, while striving to find identity within popular culture rather than exclusively outside of it.[43] According to political theorist Jonathan Dean, by 2010 few feminists were using the label "third-wave" feminist, in part because they had increasingly recognized the continuities between past and present forms of feminist activism, including the need to lobby for basic reproductive rights.[44] In contrast, the term "postfeminism" has retained its significance in both popular culture and scholarly literature, even as its precise definition remains subject to debate. The notion of "post" can, after all, indicate both the end of feminism and that which comes after or follows from it. Scholars who take issue with postfeminism argue that it amounts to a naïve rejection of feminist principles based on the false idea that gender equality has been achieved and is thus no longer a goal worth pursuing. The notion that women now have the freedom to pursue anything they choose obscures the ways in which traditionally oppressive and sexist structures continue or, according to cultural theorist Angela McRobbie, are even renewed during a contemporary period of "resurgent patriarchy."[45]

This rather bleak understanding associates postfeminism with the depoliticization of feminism and an increasing focus on individual rights, in keeping with the broader economic and cultural changes heralded by neoliberalism. In a book published in 2005, *A Brief History of Neoliberalism*, anthropologist David Harvey defines neoliberalism as a set of political and economic practices that have social effects.[46] As state intervention in the economy declines and governments increasingly eschew their responsibility to care for citizens, those citizens are expected to take personal responsibility for the conditions of their lives. Indeed, the very concept of citizenship becomes equated with self-efficacy and discipline as people are encouraged (or obliged) to regulate themselves according to the market principles of efficiency and competitiveness. While neoliberal policies shift the social burdens of poverty, illness, and unemployment into the domain of the individual, various technologies within the cultural realm, including motivational posters, talk shows, and self-help books, indirectly manage subjectivity. According to neoliberal logic, individuals are free to choose whatever lives and gendered roles they please, without contemplating oppressive structures more broadly. This situation is particularly clear within certain facets of fitness culture, which employ "fitspiration" slogans to berate those considered unfit or unhealthy, asking "What is your excuse?" or declaring "Every excuse is a decision to fail."[47] Within a neoliberal framework, anyone who is not beautiful and healthy has only him- or herself to blame.

Scholars who consider postfeminism a conformist backlash against feminism in keeping with neoliberal doctrines are critical toward rather than celebratory of various bodily practices, including the latest fitness trends, cosmetic surgery, and bodybuilding. The relatively recent practice of pole-dancing exercise classes offers a good case study of a current fitness craze. Louise Owen, a theatre and performance professor, argues that when women learn sexualized movement in relation to a "stripper's pole," they participate in the rigid reinforcement of gendered roles, advancing a spectacular kind of femininity that is tragic rather than empowering.[48] Her claims are at odds with those of gender studies scholar Samantha Holland, discussed in Chapter Two. In her ethnographic study of women who enjoy fitness pole dancing, Holland finds that they regularly report feeling more confident and liberated while working out strenuously in all-female groups.[49] These divergent conclusions are ultimately informed by the different methodologies used by the two scholars, as Owen largely considers the appearance of pole dancing and its links with burlesque, whereas Holland interviews women devoted to the practice, taking their voices as her primary source material. The feminist literature on cosmetic surgery is arguably more advanced, for it has moved beyond the oppressive/empowering paradigm to consider the ways in which cosmetic procedures are negotiated and experienced differently according to national context, among other factors.[50] Along these lines, the overview of feminist analyses of cosmetic surgery from the 1980s until 2009 offered by Cressida Heyes and Meredith Jones reconsiders both older and more recent surgical techniques, arguing that the practices are neither simply conformist nor progressive.[51] The scholarship on female bodybuilding is heading in this direction. Although much of it remains committed to evaluating representations of the built female body, Tanya Bunsell's important new research on heavyweight female bodybuilders in the United Kingdom adopts an ethnographic approach to explore how women gain strength and confidence by lifting heavier weights, ultimately finding identity within a female subculture. Without denying the sexist elements of bodybuilding competitions, Bunsell attends to the embodied experiences of female bodybuilders as they work out, navigate the spaces of the gym, and diet for upcoming shows.[52] This research focuses on the activities that dominate the women's everyday lives, rather than highlighting the few minutes they spend either onstage or posing for the camera.

My Feminist Figure Girl project finds links with Bunsell's work by emphasizing the embodied experience of bodybuilding without denying the conformist elements of figure contests, albeit from an autoethnographic rather than ethnographic perspective. Like many scholars, I entered the world of bodybuilding as an outsider, initially viewing figure competitions as displays of compliant femininity and nothing more. When I decided to explore what it felt like to train for a show, and experience it first hand, my outlook changed. This transformation was deliberate. I wanted to shake things up in both my personal and professional lives, finding new research methods that would allow me to think differently. After focusing for the better part of my career on women's intellectual capacities and human rights, seeing my feminist quest as one of defying and combating dominant culture, I sought to challenge my commitment to apparently "authentic" forms of feminist identity. The subtitle of this book, *Look Hot While You Fight the Patriarchy*, conveys the apparent contradiction of my position as well as its sense of adventure. Although meant to be provocative, even cheeky, the subtitle could also be considered offensive, especially by those who insist that feminist activism cannot take place within the confines of normative beauty culture and must occur in absolute opposition to it.

My transformation into a figure girl led me to appreciate and better understand the appeal of dominant forms of femininity, ultimately expanding my definition of feminism itself. I came to appreciate the discussion of postfeminism offered by Stéphanie Genz and Benjamin Brabon in their edited 2009 collection, *Postfeminism: Cultural Texts and Theories*.[53] After examining the manifold ways in which the term postfeminism has been used, distinguishing

between, among other things, its academic and popular understandings, they assert that postfeminism is not a political or social
movement that either counteracts or extends feminism. It is better
understood according to the definition offered by Patricia Mann, as
a "frontier discourse" that brings us to the edge of what we know,
seeking to capture the changing quality of our social, cultural, and
political experiences in the context of the more general process of
women's social enfranchisement.[54] Along these lines, postfeminism
entails standing on the edge of what we know and challenging that
knowledge. This particular description is only one among many, and
yet comes closest to expressing my interrogation of feminist principles in the Feminist Figure Girl project.

My risk-taking was enabled by multiple factors, including my
privileged position as a full professor at a prestigious university, but
was also encouraged by my movement from one place to another, from
Fredericton to Edmonton, which necessarily produced new forms of
political work, understandings of feminism, and embodied experiences. When I left Fredericton I lost a key venue for the repeated
performance of my gendered feminist self, and I wanted to recreate
it in Edmonton. Finding it impossible to duplicate that identity in
another place, I instead veered toward bodybuilding, achieving with
that practice the kind of break or rupture from my standard scripted
performance that, if I comprehend Butler correctly, might be considered subversive. At the same time, my failed performance of gender as a figure girl facilitated a new understanding of my role as a
prochoice escort. I finally realized that my prochoice work had produced a standardized identity that took shape amidst complex social
exchanges and within a particular place. It had no doubt involved
risk—the antiabortion activists repeatedly and falsely, for example,
tried to lay assault charges against me—even as it included the pleasures and perils of acting within an overtly theatrical public space.
The two forms of identity formation were thus not entirely opposed.
Both had produced concomitant forms of embodied authority, with
my in-the-streets political work at the Morgentaler Clinic providing me the credibility to speak as a feminist at rallies and with government officials, and my first-hand experience of training for and
competing in a bodybuilding show allowing me to attract readers to
my blog, give interviews to members of the media, and certify as a
personal trainer, teaching classes at my gym as well as working with

abused women at a local shelter. In both cases, I formed links with other women, creating different kinds of feminist community that could not be foreseen. In the end, my temporary transformation into a figure girl did not prevent my continued political engagement; it opened new venues for volunteer work, and in many ways marked a return to my performance of a particular gendered identity—dare I call it the role of the second-wave feminist?—with a renewed appreciation of its designated scripts and bodily gestures.

Conclusions

The two photographs that launched this discussion contain as many similarities as differences, for both show feminists enacting scripted roles within visible public spaces. Their order should nevertheless be reversed: the photograph of me posing on stage during my competition in 2011 allowed me to see the image of me shouting into a bull horn in 2007 in critical terms, as displaying more than a feminist activist delivering prochoice messages to the masses. My sideways position, relaxed posture, and loose clothing suggest a lack of interest in appearance, denying my pursuit of public spectacle, and bolstering my identity as a serious feminist activist. Comparing these photos, and confusing their "before and after" narrative, is enriching. All the same, the two images remain distinctive, depicting individual acts that occurred within particular times and places. As representations of feminist identity, the two photos are quite limited, offering mere fragments of possible forms of body politics.

In the end, the question remains: What does it feel like to be a feminist? This query is of course impossible to answer without resorting to essentialism. No feminist will have the same embodied experiences of political engagement, a point emphasized by feminist scholarship on how multiple identities are formed in relation to class, race, gender, sexuality, ability, and ethnicity, among other factors.[55] I can speak only for myself on this point, offering my account of embodied experience so that others may use it to think with, considering how theirs overlaps with or differs from mine. For me, feeling like a feminist has meant forming connections with women that are based on shared physicality, broadly understood and not biologically determined. As both a prochoice activist and a figure girl, I

FOUR

On Stage

Performing Feminist Figure Girl

"One does not infallibly stop the surge of a body that is straining towards the world and change it into a statue animated by vague tremors."
—Simone de Beauvoir[1]

In *The Second Sex*, first published in 1949, Simone de Beauvoir describes the plight of the intellectual woman, who strives to live at once like a man and a woman.[2] According to the French philosopher, this ambitious learned lady enjoys an unprecedented level of autonomy within the masculine universe that constitutes her career and yet wishes to remain obedient to womanly tradition. Her attempts to become a woman nevertheless inevitably fail, precisely because she actively seeks to adopt a feminine posture. A proper woman simply exists in the form of pure will to please; she is a "quivering object of prey."[3] In contrast, the deliberate pursuit of feminine wiles by the intellectual woman seems unsettlingly artificial.

Beauvoir notes that gendered roles were shifting by the middle of the twentieth century, making life slightly easier for the highly intelligent, career-oriented woman. Yet her discussion remains relevant today, and sheds light on my performance of Feminist Figure Girl. In the text that follows, I consider the day of the competition, which was the most theatrical public staging of my identity as a figure girl. This role necessitated a specific kind of appearance, complete with heavy makeup, hair extensions, and decorated bikini, but was also based on a series of practiced gestures. I had to walk across the stage and hold predetermined poses for what seemed like an interminably long time. My performance consisted of movement as well as stillness, transitioning between what Beauvoir calls a body that strains toward the world, animated by movement and a quest for knowledge, and one trying to mimic the stillness of a statue.

> I step out from behind the curtain and am suddenly blinded by bright stage lights. Blinking, I walk unsteadily toward the X that has been taped to the floor. My teeth are dry and sticky as I forcibly smile while hitting my presentation poses. I do my best to push my ass out and square my shoulders. The throbbing inside my head is nothing compared to the pain rising from my feet. When I finally line up with the other girls, I attempt to stand still, but my aching feet compel me to shift from side to side. Well aware that I am breaking every rule, I pray for this torture to end.

Although I never mastered walking like a woman, a failure discussed in the previous chapter, I found standing still even more difficult. On stage, dehydrated, covered in tanning dye, and with my heavy hairdo weighing down on me, I was miserable. The bony fusion in my feet, a rare birth defect, made wearing four-inch heels incredibly painful. Standing motionless in them was almost unbearable. In this chapter, I analyze my pursuit of stillness, presenting it as both a worthy goal and a point of resistance, when my body did not comply with the figure girl regime. I consider this refusal with reference to scholarly definitions of performance, introduced by a discussion of Judith Butler's arguments as presented in the previous chapter. Performance is more generally summarized by cultural theorist Amelia Jones as "the reiterative enactment across time of meaning (including that of the 'self' or subject) through embodied gestures, language, and/or other modes of signification."[4] Her account usefully highlights the themes of repetition, embodiment, time, and meaning, explored below. However, her account might also continue to privilege movement—"enactment across time"—at the expense of fixed poses, in keeping with the emphasis placed on motion by the feminist phenomenologists critiqued in Chapter Two.

I develop my analysis of performance by reflecting on works of contemporary art, drawing on my art historical training to interpret

Feminist Figure Girl. This comparative methodology was suggested by one of my colleagues, the performance artist and academic Natalie Loveless, who asked, "Is Feminist Figure Girl a work of durational performance art?" "Oh no, not at all," I immediately replied, but then paused to reflect further. I had always pictured myself as a scholar pursuing embodied research, not an artist creating something meant for an audience. Yet I ultimately decided to take my colleague's question seriously, realizing that I might have been approaching my own work too narrowly, overlooking some of its connotations.

I begin with a discussion of Marina Abramović, a Serbian-born artist who made groundbreaking work in the 1970s by using her body as her primary artistic material. Many of her early performances involved physical pain. In *Rhythm 10* (1973), for example, Abramović played a Russian game by repeatedly thrusting a sharp knife between her fingers, which were splayed open, her palm resting on a table. An audience watched as the artist cut herself, again and again.[5] During the late 1970s, Abramović began a decade-long collaboration with the German performance artist Ulay (Uwe Laysiepen), developing works that explored identity, vulnerability, and dependence on the other. In *Rest Energy* (1980), for instance, Abramović held the handle of a bow while Ulay pulled the tensed rope, armed with a sharp arrow pointing directly at her heart. Any loss of concentration or stability on his part would have had dire consequences for Abramović.[6] However, it is Abramović's more recent work that is most useful for thinking about Feminist Figure Girl. Now an established "art star," Abramović was invited to perform within the walls of the prestigious Museum of Modern Art in New York. For four months in 2010, she enacted *The Artist is Present*, remaining motionless while seated in a chair during the museum's opening hours and gazing fixedly at whoever chose to sit opposite her. Though I was unable to witness this performance, a documentary film revealed that it was a surprisingly emotional event. Some participants wept while engaging with Abramović inside the museum.[7] At one point during the documentary, Abramović declares that stillness is undervalued in our society, explaining that she seeks to teach the technique of remaining motionless to younger artists. Her insistence on the value of stillness, and the deliberate pursuit of it as a bodily practice and training method, led me to realize that my most important performance of Feminist Figure Girl had in fact occurred before I went on stage, during the disciplined preparations that had materialized time in a manner not dissimilar from the artist's own marking of days, hours, and minutes while sitting still in the Museum of Modern Art. Contemplating the work of Abramović furthermore allowed me to think about the politics of posing during my competition in new ways, drawing attention to the labor of remaining motionless, and the broader economic inflections of physical constraint within contemporary capitalist culture.

I then turn to a consideration of the art made by Canadian-born Heather Cassils, introduced in Chapter Two as a personal trainer demonstrating the effects of muscle failure. Cassils has written, "I use my exaggerated physique to intervene in various contexts in order to interrogate systems of power and control."[8] The resulting visual productions are often filmic, including such aspects as lighting, special effects, choreography, sound, and, perhaps most strikingly, the artist's highly muscled body. In a recent work called *Cuts: A Traditional Sculpture* (2011), Cassils built an already impressive physique over a period of twenty-three weeks by lifting heavy weights, consuming daily the caloric intake of a 190-pound man, and ingesting light steroids. In order to document this body as it gradually grew bigger, tighter, and harder, Cassils took four photographs of it each day, from different angles.[9] Then the artist used the still images to create a time-lapse video that shows the remarkable and shifting transformation of flesh. In this and other productions, Cassils challenges distinctions of gender while demonstrating an artistic ability to follow a regime, and shape flesh like a traditional sculptor would model clay or carve marble. Instead of the perfect male body featured in Michelangelo's canonical sculpture *David* (1501–1504), for instance, the viewer is offered a living body that defies the Renaissance ideal of masculinity even as Cassils is more male than female. The contemporary artist renders palpable the work of "doing gender," documenting and displaying the labor required to shape the body in a way that both reveals and transgresses the disciplined regulations informing contemporary fitness and beauty culture. Cassils's productions challenged me to ponder the particular effort to reproduce gender within my staging of Feminist Figure Girl, but also to consider the position of privilege I occupied, as a white heterosexual female professor, in order to do so.

Although any number of artists could have been chosen to think through my Feminist Figure Girl project, the comparisons made with Abramović and Cassils are especially fruitful. Both artists have used their own flesh as the primary medium, seeing how far they can push their bodies, and what those stressed bodies can endure over time. They have interrogated issues of stillness and movement, regularly oscillating between these states. In the end, their work allowed me to see how my creation of Feminist Figure Girl shared links with artistic acts that draw attention to the body as a medium of signification; render evident the cultural production and experience of time; and require the careful planning and repetition of set poses that are informed by, among other things, understandings of gender, sexuality, and class. Although I continue to doubt that the staging of Feminist Figure Girl was fundamentally a work of durational performance art, I am now more open to opposing arguments. Framing my research project as a work of art confirmed that my flesh had produced knowledge, and was never a site of quivering passivity. My ultimate inability to transform myself into a frozen statue of conventional femininity on stage had marked the limits of my performance, reconfirming Butler's claims that we cannot simply choose another identity, practicing and repeating its gestures to assume its substance.[10] I finally realized that I could never become a figure girl, no matter how long or how hard I tried.

Cultivating Stillness

Abramović's artistic practice has been increasingly recognized in scholarship, with monographs presenting her as the "grandmother" of performance art, and textbook surveys highlighting her place within a now substantial history of body art.[11] The lengthy and diverse career of Abramović is typically divided into phases, with early works such as *Rhythm 10* associated with themes of violence, conflict, and aggression, often involving acts of self-harm. Later works performed with Ulay shifted to investigate dependence, repetition, and endurance. In *Relation of Time* (1977), for example, the couple sat back to back, motionless, with their long hair tied together, for sixteen hours, before an audience was allowed to watch the performance during its seventeenth and final hour. Another deceptively simple immobility piece, *Nightsea Crossing*, was performed by Abramović and Ulay twelve times between 1980 and 1987. In its first manifestation at the Sydney Biennale, Ulay (dressed in red) and Abramović (dressed in black) sat still for seven hours each day, for sixteen days, gazing at each other across a table that featured objects collected during their time spent in the Australian desert, including a python and a gold-covered boomerang. In interviews, the artists explained that they had pursued corporeal stillness to exhibit the embodied condition of presence, which usually remains invisible. According to Ulay, "motionlessness is the best thing I have done. It synthesizes everything. It is the homework."[12] During these events, both Ulay and Abramović remained motionless and silent, meditating to create knowledge and exchange energy in ways informed by Tibetan Buddhism and theosophy. Stillness provided these artists with the achievement of a kind of spiritual awareness, leading them to create works infused with mysticism.

At first glance, the early works by Abramović as well as the immobility pieces she undertook with Ulay have nothing in common with my performance of Feminist Figure Girl. Although a certain degree of pain was involved in both my preparations—which included uncomfortable laser hair-removal sessions—and my onstage experience, I never actively pursued suffering or self-harm. It is true that I strove (and failed) to strike postures of immobility, holding them in ways that both recognized and attempted to overcome fleshly limitations, to a certain degree turning my body into an object. Yet my poses were held for brief moments in contrast to the extended periods of motionlessness pursued by Ulay and Abramović. Nor was there anything particularly spiritual about performing Feminist Figure Girl. Despite my rather half-hearted participation in yoga classes, discussed in the first chapter of this book, I did not embrace Eastern forms of mysticism, much less Westernized ones. I was not interested in the activity of energy exchange, described by Abramović and her partner. In fact, I never gave much thought to my audience, caring little about the actual day of the competition. It was primarily the years of planning and training, as well as the months of sustained dieting for the display held on June 4, 2011, that motivated me.

This keen attention to physical preparation is where Feminist Figure Girl finds links with the work of Ulay and especially Abramović. In 2003 Abramović founded the Independent Performance Group in Amsterdam, in part to teach students the art of self-control, taking similar ideas to her more recently established Foundation for Preservation of Performance Art in Hudson, New York.[13] Abramović's followers regularly observe rigid rules designed to regulate and highlight embodiment. For measured periods—sometimes days on end—her trainees must refrain from eating, speaking, engaging in sexual activity, and from such forms of entertainment as watching television, reading books, or writing. The senior artist explained that this kind of regime, including fasting, was liable to test the students' motivation while forcing them to experience sensual deprivation, which would ultimately render them physically weaker but mentally transformed and more focused afterward.[14] Shorter exercises could produce similar results, and Abramović described how "taking a bath in the ice-cold water of the river or sea, [could help] us reinforce our physical strength."[15] Overall, then, Abramović's workshops were (and still are) meant to teach participants endurance, concentration, mindfulness, perception, self-control, and willpower, while compelling them to confront their mental and physical limits. No longer concerned with the experience or display of pain, the artist refuses to mentor students with eating disorders or those who take prescription drugs, are depressed, or pursue acts of self-destruction.[16]

The methods and outcomes endorsed by Abramović overlap in significant ways with those promoted officially within the bodybuilding and figure girl subcultures. Preparing to compete on stage is largely ritualistic, with participants following set protocols, and passing through various levels: they bulk up by building muscle and then diet down to lose fat; drink liters of water the week before a show and then deliberately dehydrate the body in order to look "tight" on stage; restrict carbohydrate and fat consumption for months before a competition and then carb- and fat-load during the final week, so as to appear "full" while posing under the hot stage lights. According to my personal experiences, conversations at the gym, and a publication called *Figure Competition Secrets* by Karen Sessions, the goal of enduring these rituals is to "bring your best" to the stage, reaping such rewards as a sense of accomplishment and social respect for hard work made visible.[17] A competitor will gain esteem from other members of the bodybuilding community by successfully navigating these timed physical rituals and adopting the appropriate aesthetic on stage. Although this final display is only the capstone of a lengthy and often grueling process, it is difficult—I would say impossible—to claim to be either a bodybuilder or a figure girl without participating in at least one show.[18]

Competing in such contests might appear to be fueled by misguided narcissism, but all of the women who spoke with me backstage during my own competition in Edmonton viewed competing as a test. These figure girls affirmed that they had passed the test by enduring the months of rigid preparation required to look muscular and lean on stage. The contestants who reported being unhappy with themselves had "cheated;" that is, they had skipped their cardio sessions or eaten more foods than those allotted by their diet coaches, making them appear to be "fat," "soft," or "skinny," all equally undesirable conditions. One satisfied participant confided that she had entered a figure competition to help her overcome an eating disorder.[19] Consuming six high-protein meals per day on her precompetition diet had allowed her to gain weight, at odds with her former addiction to anorexia. However, success in the world of figure and bodybuilding competitions does not usually involve such extremes. It requires a consistent dedication to a set of bodily regimes, patterns, and movements, in a manner not dissimilar from the exercises promoted by Abramović. To a certain degree the desired results of having competed in a bodybuilding or figure show also overlap with those endorsed by the artist: the acquisition of self-knowledge, the ability to push against bodily limitations, the pursuit of novel and potentially uncomfortable physical sensations, and the accumulation of accomplishments from which to draw strength for future endeavors.

My own precompetition preparation rituals were strangely congruent with Abramović's training regime—I was even submerged underwater to have my body fat tested, a torturous experience described in Chapter One—but her use of food-management techniques is especially striking. The artist seems to focus on abstention and physical denial in a way that is reminiscent of the practices of some medieval holy women, intent on fleshly suffering in an effort to imitate Christ.[20] For Abramović, the restriction of food intake is meant to encourage her students to attend to the body, in order both to acknowledge the power of and master its demands. Along the same lines, the careful regulation of food intake is one of the most important aspects of preparing for a figure competition, and is certainly considered the most challenging part of the process by most participants. A standard figure or bodybuilding diet does not, however, feature deprivation per se. I ate a large quantity of food during the first month of my diet, though the amounts and precise foods noted below changed significantly as the competition date drew closer. During the third week of January 2011, I consumed the following on a daily basis: 100 grams of butternut squash, 60 grams of baked sweet potato, 50 grams of dry oatmeal, one half cup of skim milk, 215 grams of Brussels sprouts, one scoop of protein powder, 25 grams of almonds, 115 grams of basa fish, 170 grams of buffalo meat, 140 grams of chicken breast, and 8 egg whites. This diet regime did not induce hunger; it necessitated a highly organized lifestyle, based on the continual preparation of food, which was then precisely measured and consumed at timed intervals. To a significant degree, becoming a figure girl required the skills of time management as much as, or even more than, those of physical control. My precompetition days were marked by regular alerts from my cell phone, reminding me to take my vitamins and other supplements, and by my continual reference to the diet instructions I had printed and taped to a wall in my kitchen.

In keeping with Abramović's methods, the figure girl regime cultivates and values discipline. It deliberately undermines established bodily habits to allow for the creation of new ones. During the five months that preceded my competition, I reshaped my body, not only by eating and taking supplements every few hours but by adhering to a rigid training schedule—I worked shoulders on Monday, hamstrings and glutes on Tuesday, back on Wednesday, arms on Thursday, quads on Friday, and did an hour or more of cardio every day—and by making regular visits to the tanning salon, massage therapist, and hair salon, where my longtime stylist was gradually turning my dark hair blonde. This sustained and rigid pattern might remind some readers of a passage from Michel Foucault's book *Discipline and Punish*, in which the historian and philosopher describes the regulated day of an early nineteenth-century French prisoner: he rose at 6 a.m., dressed and made his bed by 6:05, lined up for prayers at 6:10, went to the courtyard to wash at 6:45, and so forth, end-lessly.[21] Foucault explains that the adoption of this particular econ-omy of punishment and rejection of the previous practice of public execution was not motivated by a desire to treat inmates in a more humane fashion. The strict management of the physical activities of prisoners was instituted because it was an efficient method of render-ing their bodies more docile and malleable. In many ways, the figure girl training methods and the exercises advocated by Abramović are similarly designed to materialize the living body so that it can be reshaped into an ideal or at least different form. But are these bodies meant to become more or less governable? More or less productive?

Both Abramović's method and the standard figure girl regime involve a willing submission to restraint, with adherents follow-ing the directions provided by authorities. Abramović overtly takes up the role of leader and role model while guiding her students to greater mindfulness and self-realization. In contrast, while preparing for my competition, I temporarily relinquished the role of an author-ity figure and became a follower, setting to one side my identity as a professor to purchase the services of those more knowledgeable than me in the practice and performance of bodybuilding. I hired a diet coach named Raejha Douziech, a former professional bodybuilder and figure champion, who also led me through a series of much-needed posing lessons. I relied on my personal trainer, Audrey Shep-herd, to provide me with a weight-lifting program, and to guide me through workouts twice a week during the precompetition period. I also drew on the skills of my hair dresser, various laser hair-removal technicians, and a makeup artist on the day of my competition. I deliberately did not question or challenge any of these authorities, even when I was not particularly pleased by their directions. When my diet coach told me, for instance, that my chest and midback were too muscular for an ideal figure girl body, I complied with her instructions to stop training them with heavy weights. I understood my role in the process to be one of submission and obedience, will-ingly taking up what was for me a novel stance.

Despite significant overlaps, the intentions of the students who agreed to obey Abramović nevertheless were (and remain) rather different from my own. In theory at least, her physical practices encourage novice performance artists to become more present and live in the moment while communicating meanings to audiences in a direct, authentic manner. This emphasis on presence, including how it is defined, developed, and experienced, is of great interest to practicing performance artists and within scholarship about performance art.[22] The Abramović method promotes a particular version of presence by encouraging adherents to reject the dominant mode of being in the world by refusing to be distracted, unaware, and disembodied consumers of pleasure. In contrast, my adherence to a rather standard figure girl regime was primarily designed to make me conform to a physical ideal within that subculture, one that favors defined shoulder caps, small waists, and developed quad muscles. Becoming a figure girl has little to do with the pursuit of mental alertness, mindfulness, or living in the moment. My mental capacities were in fact diminished by an exhausting daily routine that was entirely geared toward the future, not any form of presence. While the exercises developed by Abramović might succeed in reshaping bodies in order to "free" them from a dominant norm, I found that the figure girl regime is more likely to render its followers increasingly conformist, moving them closer to mindless consumption rather than toward a point of social or cultural resistance.

I spent a ridiculous amount of money preparing for my onstage display. By striving to become a figure girl I necessarily became a model consumer, focusing on body, hair, skin, and nail care products in a way previously unknown to me. In addition to purchasing the services of the experts noted above, I paid $800 for a custom-made bikini, bought three pairs of special posing shoes, and made weekly treks to an organic butcher to order massive amounts of bison meat, among dozens of other expenditures that I am reluctant to spell out. This project was not funded by grants because I feared being hindered by their requirements, so my line of credit took quite a hit. My comfortable position as a full professor on sabbatical enabled me to afford these items, "bringing my best" to the stage without needing to cut any corners, a luxury enjoyed by few other figure girls. Initially I justified my mounting bills as research expenses, but my encounter with Abramović's work in New York forced me to reconsider the economic aspects of my staging of Feminist Figure Girl.

One of the most striking and effective aspects of Abramović's performance within the Museum of Modern Art was the way in which she drew attention to the work of being an artist. Her presence

Figure 4.1. Shelby Lessig photo of Marina Abramović performing *The Artist is Present* at the Museum of Modern Art in May 2010 (courtesy of Shelby Lessig, Creative Commons Attribution-Share Alike License).

there was arguably unsettling, challenging both the normal functioning of the museum and the longstanding definition of such institutions as temples devoted to the acquisition and display of valuable art objects. While I appreciate the radical potential of *The Artist is Present*, which brought many first-time visitors into the Museum of Modern Art for a direct experience of the artist's body, others have accused Abramović of "selling out" by commodifying her international reputation in a manner that ultimately enhanced the longstanding authority of the museum.[23] All the same, I insist that her intervention was successful because she made artistic labor visible. Abramović was consistently present in the museum during its opening hours, almost punching a clock as would an employee. While her willing submission to corporeal restraint and voluntary performance of emotional labor might reinforce the stereotype of the sacrificial artist, who gives body and soul to his [sic] work, it also linked her artistic production with various forms of waged labor. The working day of many people involves a similar regime of bodily control, requiring them to remain seated at a desk, focused on a computer screen, or to adopt a pleasant demeanor when interacting with the public, albeit with timed bathroom and lunch breaks, in contrast to Abramović's sustained stillness.[24] With her performance of *The Artist is Present*, Abramović invited audiences to contemplate, among other things, the significance of physical and emotional restraint in their own lives and, by extension, in contemporary Western culture more generally. It certainly encouraged me to examine the economy of labor, as well as the tension between stillness and movement, in my own profession and ongoing research project.

The regime of a professor demands significant periods of relative stillness while hunching over a computer keyboard or intensely grading a pile of exams. Both the physical and intellectual demands of this profession usually remain invisible to nonacademics, and are rarely displayed in public venues. It was therefore rewarding for me when the hard work of growing muscle became increasingly visible—attracting appreciative comments at the gym—as I lost fat in order to take to the stage as Feminist Figure Girl. This validating experience nevertheless involved my submission to a constraining routine and concomitant loss of autonomy. Before I started training for a bodybuilding competition, I had moved freely throughout my day, enjoying flexible time despite working at least fifty hours per week, a number that increased to about seventy during the five months preceding my competition. For the most part, my profession had allowed me to decide when and where to work, without requiring the kind of emotional labor more closely associated with service industry positions of lower social status. My work as a professor had also included regular travel to deliver papers, attend conferences, and participate in art openings. This kind of mobility became more difficult during my precompetition period. In February 2011, some four months before my show, I was invited, for example, to give a talk about the seventeenth-century illnesses of the French King Louis XIV to medical students at the University of Ottawa. Eschewing the planned receptions and dinners, I cooked, weighed, and packed four days' worth of diet food, filling my luggage with small plastic containers of fibrous vegetables and meat, wolfing them down between meetings or in restaurant bathrooms while in Ottawa. My ability to travel and to engage in the social situations that are a key part of my career were seriously hindered by my competing identity as a figure girl, a role that curtailed my liberty while highlighting the privileges I enjoyed as a professor. I did not arrive, however, at a more

extensive understanding of the politics of labor, mobility, and stillness involved in my staging of Feminist Figure Girl until I encountered the artistic productions of Heather Cassils.

Transforming Labor

Despite the significant areas of convergence between the work of
Abramović and my own endeavors, it was more rewarding to compare Feminist Figure Girl with the creations of Heather Cassils, particularly the multiple results of the durational project called *Cuts: A
Traditional Sculpture*, described above. This project formed the basis
of, among other images, a time-lapse video that condensed Cassils's
twenty-three-week muscle building project into twenty-three seconds, showing how the artist's body had changed over time (www.
heathercassils.com). The video both speeds up time to portray Cassils literally growing bigger, and slows down to focus on the labor
that produced this result. Instead of revealing work in terms of concentrated stillness, like Abramović, the slowed scenes portray Cassils
pushing and pulling heavy weights, and ripping a roast chicken apart
with bare hands, alluding to the aggressively large quantities of protein that the human body must process in order to develop substantial muscle mass. Overall, the video reveals that Cassils achieved a
"hypermasculine" body by following a rather traditional bodybuilding regimen—administered by Charles Glass, a former professional
bodybuilder and renowned trainer, and David Kalick, a nutritionist
specializing in diets for athletes—resembling my own precompetition routine in both its duration and content.[25]

I identified with many aspects of Cassils's project, immediately
recognizing its glorification of physical effort and determination. I
felt that I had special insight when interpreting the artist's facial
expressions, which ranged from grimaces of determination while
lifting impossibly heavy weights to the less intense signs of placid
resignation when robotically consuming food as a required chore
rather than in response to hunger or desire. Most of all, I could discern the exhaustion etched across Cassils's features. Seeing Cassils's
blank eyes with lids half closed beneath a furrowed brow was like
looking into a mirror during the last few months before my competition. I too was visibly tired, no longer able to walk up the three

flights of stairs to my condo or make the twenty-minute trek to my gym, even as I relentlessly continued to train and do cardio every single day.

Both Cassils and I had pursued a physical goal, one primarily represented by means of digital technologies. The artist produced daily photographs that were ultimately animated to make corporeal change palpable in video form, and, at the end of the twenty-three-week process, had a series of still images produced of the finished sculpture/body.[26] I too had participated in the regular documentation of my physical transformation. Every Friday morning, after going to the bathroom and before drinking two cups of lemon-infused water, I would weigh myself and then pose in a string bikini while my partner took photographs of me from the front, back, and both sides. I would then e-mail my weight and these images to my diet coach, awaiting her evaluation of them, which usually came in the form of an altered food regimen for the following week or an increase in the length of my daily cardio sessions. Yet I neglected to save these photographs systematically, in part because they had a practical and immediate function. I nevertheless retained hundreds of other pictures of me from this period, taken during training sessions, while preparing food, and, most of all, during the competition itself, when I was on stage. To a large degree, figure contests are designed to produce images, usually still photographs of competitors dressed in their custom-fitted posing suits, with hair and makeup professionally done. I analyze the function and status of photography within the Feminist Figure Girl project in the next chapter, drawing attention to the ways in which I participated in and tried to subvert this representational practice. Here I want primarily to point out the many connections between Cassils's *Cuts* and my own project, especially in terms of process, setting the stage for a comparison of the still images of our "finished product."

All the same, Cassils deliberately made a work of art, whereas I required prompting to consider the artistic potential of Feminist Figure Girl, and only did so belatedly. The title of Cassils's project, *Cuts*, alludes to filmmaking, while its subtitle, *A Traditional Sculpture*, frames the project within the history of art. This reference also invokes an influential feminist work made by Eleanor Antin between 15 July and 21 August, 1972, called *Carving: A Traditional Sculpture*.[27] While following a strict weight-loss regimen for

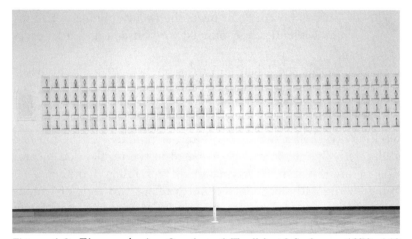

Figure 4.2. Eleanor Antin, *Carving: A Traditional Sculpture*, 1972, 148 gelatin prints and text panel, each photograph 17.7 x 12.7 cm., text panel 39.4 x 26 cm. Twentieth-Century Discretionary Fund, 1996.44, The Art Institute of Chicago.

thirty-seven days, Antin was photographed every morning standing naked in four positions: from the front, back, and both sides. The installation of her completed work consisted of 148 of these black and white images, arranged chronologically in rows to allow viewers to scrutinize and assess the transformation of her flesh while potentially reflecting on the construction of ideal femininity as passive and objectified. Antin's reference to sculptural tradition furthermore invokes the working methods of ancient Greek carvers, who approached a marble block from all sides, as if releasing the figure already inside it, an understanding of sculptural practice also espoused by Michelangelo.[28] In keeping with her predecessors' respect for the agency of materiality—it can be reshaped by following learned regulations, within limited parameters—Antin revealed that the human body is material, at once changeable and yet not entirely subject to mastery. Cassils adopts a similar approach to corporeality but reverses the process by growing bigger and actively pursuing a masculine position. The finished products drawn from *Cuts: A Traditional Sculpture* thus offer more than a commentary on Antin's original piece, or an elaboration of its feminist content.

In one of the striking pin-up images produced at the end of the project—it was featured in the zine called *Lady Face//Man Body*,

Figure 4.3. Heather Cassils, "Advertisement: Homage to Benglis with Tabloid Grid," photograph by Heather Cassils and Robin Black, 2011. Part of a larger body of work: *Cuts: A Traditional Sculpture.* (Image Courtesy of Ronald Feldman Fine Arts.)

made collaboratively with photographer Robin Black—Cassils is shown looking ripped and hard, after having gained twenty-three pounds of muscle by sculpting flesh through bodybuilding.[29] Adopting the frontal pose of an anatomical figure, the artist offers the resulting fat-free body for the appraisal of an audience. The image features professional lighting and saturated color, showing the rippled muscles and vascularity of a model sporting a white jock strap and full makeup, including bright red lipstick. The theatrical aspects of this image contrast with the unadorned, black and white presentation of Antin. Shown entirely nude and standing in a relaxed posture, Antin's images combine the aesthetics of documentary and medical photography, purporting to offer viewers a direct demonstration of what had happened to her body. In contrast, the pin-up photograph of Cassils is more assertive, not only because of the tensed muscles that connote energy and potential movement, but also because it includes signs of the deliberate alteration of appearance; the model has styled hair, wears noticeable rather than "natural" makeup, and has a prominent phallic bulge. Cassils is "packing," adorned with the signifiers of both femininity and masculinity. While Antin questions the nature of the female body, Cassils includes a critique of masculinity, undermining gendered binaries in a way that defies them instead of merely pointing to them.

Both the theatrical aesthetic and prominent phallus in Cassils' pin-up photograph are in dialogue with another canonical work of feminist art, namely the advertisements that Lynda Benglis had published in *Artforum* magazine in 1974.[30] Benglis had posed naked, her lithe body marked by visible tan lines, with one hand on her hip and the other holding a long dildo against her vulva. By paying to have this image published in a respected art journal, the artist had offered a critique of the male-dominated art world, which marginalized female artists and ignored her own sculptural productions. In the advertisement, Benglis adopts an aggressive stance by looking directly at her audience—albeit with eyes hidden by movie star sunglasses—and brandishing an artificial penis (see a reproduction of this image at www.heathercassils.com—click on "Cuts: A Traditional Sculpture" and then scroll all the way down to the last image). Instead of drawing attention to the objectification and ideal passivity of the female body like Antin, Benglis mimics a posture of female sexual display from mainstream pornography, while compensating for her supposed physical deficiency by flagrantly adding a temporary penis. Benglis offers the dildo as a fetish object, which, according to Freudian theory, at once recognizes and denies women's bodily lack in an effort to manage castration anxiety.[31] With this photograph, Benglis insisted on the misogynistic fears and irrationality then driving the established art world, offering a "fuck you" message to those participating in it. The resulting image was upsetting to many viewers when it was first published in *Artforum* because it revealed that a penis was at once necessary in order to be awarded artistic merit, as well as ridiculously superfluous.

Cassils's display of a masculinized body also unsettled a number of viewers—one comment on YouTube calls the project "disgusting"—while attracting the admiration of many others.[32] Yet in contrast to the presentations of both Benglis and Antin, Cassils is never fully naked in any of the images produced from *Cuts: A Traditional Sculpture*; the genital area is always covered. In the pin-up image from the zine *Lady Face//Man Body*, a penis is both present and absent in the bulging cloth of the jock strap. This signifier of

Figure 4.4. Heather Cassils, "Advertisement: Homage to Benglis," photograph by Heather Cassils and Robin Black, 2011. Part of a larger body of work: *Cuts: A Traditional Sculpture.* (Image Courtesy of Ronald Feldman Fine Arts.)

masculinity is uncertain and potentially confusing to viewers, a point highlighted by the reactions to its reproduction in a poster that I distributed at the gym to advertise a talk that Cassils was invited to give at the University of Alberta in November 2012. One male participant in my spin class looked closely at the representation of Cassils, expressed interest in the artwork, and then pointed directly at the phallic bulge before asking, "What is going on here?" "Come to the artist's lecture and you might find out," I responded. During the talk later that week, Cassils did indeed address this issue, explaining that the crotch area was covered in this and other images because audiences tended to become fixated on that region, overlooking other information. Concealing this part of the body at once recognized and refused to allow their commonplace efforts to fix the model's identity and determine its meaning.

Another image from Cassils's zine similarly plays with the assumption that the epistemological basis for secure knowledge about the body can be found in a visual analysis and categorization of its genitalia. In this case, the photographer has selected a fragment of the artist's body, zooming in on the area located between the lower torso and above the knees. Instead of clothing, Cassils's hands conceal the pubic region, with palms facing each other to suggest a vulva and thumbs pointed outward in the form of a clitoris or small penis. This body is indeterminate, carrying signifiers of both the male and female. As Cassils's hands fabricate this duality, they portray the body itself as an artistic medium, displacing the paint brushes and chisels often held by artists in the self-portraits they produced as forms of self-promotion and display from the fifteenth century on.[33] In the contemporary image, Cassils's bare hands are at work producing arguments about the self, shown tensed in a bodybuilding pose designed to flex the body and display its "shredded" or "cut" condition, making individual muscles and veins even more visible. This particular image of Cassils's body thus offers a compressed version of *Cuts: A Traditional Sculpture*: bodybuilding is the method used by a working artist to reshape the body, revealing that flesh is essentially a cultural medium, not a natural entity that pre-exists the subject or is fundamentally able to provide factual information about it.

Flesh nevertheless has agency in Cassils's work. It fails to perform another repetition, grows tired, requires fuel, and cannot be fully constrained by such signifiers of gender as dress and adornment. One notable scene in the time-lapse video slows down to focus on the artist's wide back as it swells to shred, Hulk-style, a white shirt that used to fit. Even as this body is shaped by and

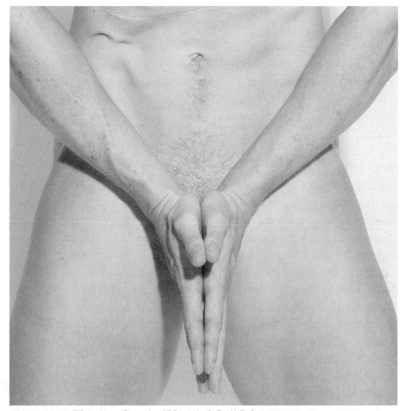

Figure 4.5. Heather Cassils, "Untitled Still," from *Lady Face // Man Body* publication, photograph by Heather Cassils and Robin Black, 2011. (Image Courtesy of Ronald Feldman Fine Arts.)

measured in relation to the shirt, it can insistently expand beyond it. The dynamic relationship between clothing and musculature has been explored by a number of scholars, including the competitive bodybuilder Marcia Ian. [34] She argues that muscles are a form of dress because we fabricate and wear them as part of the presentation of self. According to Ian, the act of heavyweight bodybuilding renders evident the body-as-costume, revealing the fluidity of the subject in a manner that is frightening for some, empowering for others. Bodybuilding suggests that human flesh is temporary and changeable, an unwelcome reminder of mortality for many viewers of hypermuscular frames. All the same, the body has limits and cannot really be molded like clay, or simply be put on and taken off like clothing. It can be obdurate in a way that resists change and refuses to allow mastery.

This combination of signs of mutability with those of insistent materiality is crucial to Cassils's representation of trans identity. The artist uses bodybuilding to undermine categories that are usually opposed, bringing together male/female, masculine/feminine, nature/culture, and sex/gender to embrace multiplicity and ambiguity. In contemporary Western culture, a body with visible musculature can send confusing and contradictory messages, a situation explored and arguably enjoyed by Cassils as well as Ian. While musculature remains for the most part coded as male or masculine, Ian contends that when muscles are exaggerated in size they become strangely ungendered, enacting a "revenge against sex" by turning each practitioner's veiny, engorged body into something resembling a giant penis.[35] On one hand, this transformation recognizes the inadequacy of the "natural" penis, which does not deserve the privileges awarded to it. On the other hand, it allows subjects categorized as female to move into the male domain, potentially shedding the negative connotations of femininity. According to Ian, competitive female bodybuilders like her "strive to embody in their own disciplined flesh all the clichés of masculinism from the barbarous to the sublime. Female bodybuilders do this not because they want to be men, but because, like men, they want to eradicate from themselves their sentimentalized 'femininity,' and its historical equivalent, immanent passivity."[36] This debatable conception of the male-identified, phallic bodybuilder could shed some light on why the pin-up image of Cassils does not need to include either a fleshly appendage or an artificially removable one like that of Benglis. Yet Cassils's muscularity is not so easily classified as phallic, for when certain viewers regard images of the artist's inflated male body, they see the other, apparently competing signs of gender, like lipstick and bra tan-lines, and then look in confusion toward the crotch area to fix the subject's identity. This search for definitive visual proof is continually thwarted by the representations of Cassils, a situation that can be experienced as pleasurable, intriguing, or frustrating, depending on the viewer's inclinations.

Cassils contributes to the recently institutionalized field of trans studies (sometimes called transgender studies) and to the more longstanding realm of trans activism.[37] Instead of emphasizing issues of trans community, citizenship, legal rights, or historical precedent, however, the artist promotes bodybuilding as a fundamentally trans activity. The practice of bodybuilding is often discussed by scholars as either gender bending or gender regulating. Among other things, bodybuilding places macho men in poses of feminine display and requires large manly women to counteract their threatening appearance with such signifiers of femininity as blonde hair, heavy makeup, and painted fingernails.[38] Bodybuilding is also regularly labeled a queer practice, embraced by gay men in an effort to attain a particular aesthetic, or else liable to incite homoerotic and/or homophobic responses both in and out of the gym.[39] Even as these discussions address the mixed messages and potential gender confusion created by bodybuilding, they tend to ignore the fleshly impact and embodied experience of lifting heavy weights. The deliberate growth of muscle can, for example, increase the amount of testosterone in a practitioner's body, which then causes a concomitant increase in certain types of estrogen; both estrogens and androgens are produced in all bodies to varying degrees.[40] When male bodybuilders enhance the amount of testosterone in their bodies by injecting anabolic-androgenic steroids, they will likely become more muscular and more conventionally manly, but can also show signs of supposed "femaleness" at sites that convert testosterone into estrogen, resulting in fatty deposits around their nipples, otherwise known as gynecomastia, or more colloquially as "bitch tits." When female bodybuilders take anavar, a light oral steroid, they increase their level of testosterone and thereby enhance muscle growth, but also enlarge their clitoris, an often welcomed condition known as "var-clit" within the bodybuilding subculture. Extensive use of anavar or more substantial anabolic-androgenic steroids will also cause women to have a lowered voice, increased amount of facial hair, and enlarged pores in their skin. Understanding that bodybuilding reveals how human bodies can be both male and female, Cassils draws on an extensive physiological knowledge and personal experience to create images that demonstrate how the masculinized body is accordingly feminized, with a single or "correct" designation neither easy to discern nor stable over time.

Although I had read about and looked at selections from *Cuts: A Traditional Sculpture* online, I did not engage with the visual complexity of Cassils's work until the artist was at the University of

Alberta. As I sat in the audience, watching the videos and listening to the talk, I reconsidered the goals of my own bodybuilding project, finding them initially similar to and then radically different from those of Cassils. I decided that the intentions of Feminist Figure Girl had paled in contrast to Cassils's allusion to layers of artistic tradition, multiple forms of popular culture, including fashion magazines, gay pornography, and zines, and the representation of trans identity. How could a similar richness be offered by a mostly female-identified, heterosexual woman who had entered a figure competition in order to see how it felt to conform rigidly to feminine conventions? By someone who had willingly embraced the capitalist economy of desire for youth and female beauty? I pondered the compliments that I regularly received for my "courage" in pursuing the Feminist Figure Girl project, reconfirming my rejection of them. After all, how dangerous could it have been for a full, tenured professor to wear high heels and a bikini on stage? Who on earth would be made uncomfortable by such a spectacle?

Then I remembered that many people had in fact become alarmed and were even disgusted by my display. During the final two months before my competition, when I was visibly muscular and lean, I had faced resistance on a daily basis, mainly from colleagues, friends, and acquaintances, who inquired about my "unhealthy" project, wondering if I had "gone too far." While these questions were presumably motivated by sincere concern, I was subject to outright attack after the images of me on stage were published both in print and online in newspapers across Canada in late June 2011. Anonymous commentators asked, "Why would a women [sic] want to have the body of a man?" "How is this femenine? [sic]. She looks like a male bodybuilder."[41] Other responses to my image insisted that I was a man-hating lesbian who (ironically?) wanted to look like a man, and would "die an old bitter spinster." More than a few questioned my ability to conceive and bear children, wondering if I was even able to menstruate.[42] While there were an equal number of positive comments, mostly congratulating me for my discipline and bravado, the negative ones were more interesting to me. They were also more surprising, for in my opinion while on stage I had never looked more conservatively lady like, displaying my body for a panel of male judges while wearing a tiny bikini, delicate jewelry, heavy

Figure 4.6. David Ford photograph of Lianne McTavish on stage at 2011 Northern Alberta Bodybuilding Championships, Edmonton, Alberta, Tier I Figure (Medium) and Masters Figure Divisions (courtesy of Lianne McTavish).

makeup, hair extensions, and high heels for the first time in my life. Yet it seems that many outraged viewers had easily overlooked all of these gendered signifiers; these signs of femininity had in effect been overruled by my "manly" musculature, which sent mixed messages that were apparently disturbing and definitely perceived as contradictory.

The sheer persistence of biological essentialism was palpable in these responses, as was the narrowness of current gender roles. Even though I had lost muscle in my chest and midback, becoming softer in order to take the stage as a figure girl, I was perceived as transgressive and in need of gender policing. This response to my performance of Feminist Figure Girl counteracts the arguments made by avid weight lifter and cultural critic Anne Bolin, who contends that figure competitions feature women with soft nonmuscular bodies that are meant to counteract the threat of female heavyweight bodybuilders.[43] Apparently, even the smaller figure girls are still too muscular and hard for the "general population" to bear. The supposed manliness of my body was largely conflated with the visibility of my musculature, ribs, and veins, lending credence to Pamela L. Moore's observation that female bodybuilders are like flayed anatomical figures, displaying the interior of the body instead of maintaining a mysteriously "feminine" hidden core.[44] A number of the critical comments directed at my staged photograph objected to my lack of maternal features, which they seemed to equate with body fat, overtly noting that I had deficient tits and ass, and others went further by implying that my internal reproductive organs were equally absent. To them I had created something ridiculously monstrous, asexual, and sterile.

Despite taking umbrage at these criticisms, I never had to fear for my personal safety or that I would be stripped of my civil rights, as do trans people and other gender outlaws. I nevertheless had to agree that I had failed in my quest for gender conformity. The photograph that some viewers found offensive had captured a stillness that had in fact never existed, for I was unable to hold the requisite figure girl poses while on stage. Although I had dressed for the part, in the end I did not deliver the "complete package," and instead felt the weight of my body's refusal to comply fully with the demands of the figure girl regime. I found it fascinating that my precompetition preparations had emphasized movement and constant change, but my final display was primarily meant to "freeze" my body, creating an object to be scrutinized. In order to think about this situation, I turned once again to the work of Cassils. This artist had elaborated on the sheer labor of posing, and ultimate inability to fix the body in one place, in a cinematic work called *Hard Times* (2010), adopting the look of a female bodybuilder, complete with ripped physique, dark tan, extravagant blonde wig, and coral posing suit.[45] After donning this costume, Cassils attempted to maintain bodybuilding poses in a slow and controlled way while teetering seven feet above the audience on top of a slippery piece of plywood barely supported by unstable scaffolding. Holding these poses was physically impossible, not only because of the insecure platform but also because the stress of maintaining deep muscular contractions overloads the nervous system and produces muscle spasms. While shaking uncontrollably, Cassils revealed the material constraints of the body while alluding to the "production and effort that goes into upholding a superficial image."[46] The artist furthermore linked the stressed body with concurrent economic conditions, the "hard times" faced by friends and colleagues who were continually working and yet unable to achieve their desired standard of living. More broadly, Cassils commented on the decline of capitalism, which people struggle to maintain in the face of its destruction from within. Caught up in economic failure, many Americans as well as other inhabitants of the Western world remain committed to supporting a system that is demonstrably unsustainable.[47]

As I sat in the audience at the University of Alberta listening to Cassils explain *Hard Times*, I recalled another critique of the imbrication of bodies and capitalism, namely the one offered by cultural critic Lauren Berlant in her book *Cruel Optimism* (2011). The author defines cruel optimism as a "relation that exists when something you desire is actually an obstacle to your flourishing," theorizing about how and why people live this relation.[48] Tracking the affective attachment to what contemporary Western capitalist and consumer culture has characterized as "the good life," Berlant notes that this conception simultaneously enables subjects to exist and wears them down. Among other conditions, she analyzes the slow death caused by the so-called obesity epidemic, which negatively affects minority

Figure 4.7. Heather Cassils, "Hard Times: Performance Still," photograph by Clover Leary, 2009. (Image Courtesy of Ronald Feldman Fine Arts.)

and oppressed populations even as members of those populations find solace in food consumption as an accessible form of pleasure and reliable basis for social cohesion.[49] Thinking along these lines, I decided that, for me, posing was a specific kind of cruel optimism; during my posing practice sessions I had repeatedly failed to perform like a figure girl, but I had nevertheless clung to the belief that I would triumphantly succeed on stage. All the same, my decision to pursue stillness and restraint as a novel research opportunity was made possible by the privilege of my professorial mobility. Other workers are subject to constraining postures without such apparent consent. Physical stress is not usually experienced as a choice but rather as an obligatory burden in the quest for the elusive "good life." I was able to stress my body, driving it to its limits, in my Feminist Figure Girl project, because the platform on which I was standing was secure, at least for the time being.

This account nevertheless overstates my agency, a presumption that was challenged when my body refused to assume the pose of a figure girl on stage. Despite conforming to my workout and diet regimen, in the end my flesh was recalcitrant, making itself palpably present on stage in a way that all could see. This body (i.e., myself) exposed the hard work of posing as a subject; that is, it exposed the labor of preparing to stay still and then attempting to do so again and again, in dialogue with the artistic productions of Abramović and Cassils. While on stage my body offered a lesson about the unceasing effort involved both in becoming a woman and transforming into a figure girl, revealing the impossibility of achieving these roles. My repeated attempts to pose ultimately confirmed the arguments about gendered performance made by Judith Butler, who insists that bodies do not exist prior to their marking by gender but are instead compelled to embody historically and culturally specific norms.[50] Repetition of these norms over time creates meaning, instantiating them in the body even as each reiteration differs from the previous one. My stressed and shaking body made material the necessarily continuous performance of gender, and the instability of gendered categories. At the same time, my failure to pose as a figure girl indicated that while new forms of embodiment are worth pursuing for educational and political purposes, they cannot really be chosen or arbitrarily adopted at will.

Conclusions

Simone de Beauvoir was correct to state that a body straining toward the world cannot suddenly be reshaped into a statue. Like the intellectual woman who fails to perform as a woman because she is trying too hard, the artificiality of my performance as a figure girl was disturbing to some viewers. My active pursuit of passivity was bound to fail. All the same, Beauvoir's conflation of movement with knowledge is open to question, for stillness, or at least my attempt to achieve it, was worthwhile, leading to the production of new insights about embodiment, gender, and performance. The work of artist Marina Abramović helpfully suggested that the disciplined cultivation of motionlessness could offer a path of resistance to the contemporary mode of being in the world. During my onstage enactment of Feminist Figure Girl, the quest for stillness had indeed produced a point of rupture, where my carefully crafted image had dissolved, opening a fissure to reveal the highly constructed nature of my practice and obdurate materiality of my historically and culturally produced flesh.

The Feminist Figure Girl project shared many qualities with contemporary performance art by materializing time, displaying a body under stress before an audience, and engaging with such issues as embodiment, gender, sexuality, difference, and ephemerality. Though I cannot claim the title of artist, much less of performance artist, my work was enriched by its comparison with that of Abramović and Cassils. Abramović enabled me to see that my disciplined precompetition rituals were important instances of performance, shifting my attention away from the supposedly penultimate moment on stage while forcing me to think about the economic conditions that had produced it. Cassils encouraged me to analyze staging itself, particularly in terms of the posing required in bodybuilding and, more important, the construction of a subject that repetitively attempts to fix identity and thereby ensures its instability.

Like a performance artist, I took my body as primary research material, learning about the vulnerability, variableness, and limits of flesh. This process by no means positioned the body as a site of origin, or as ultimately other than culture. On the contrary, the Feminist Figure Girl regime confirmed Butler's contention that the body's intelligibility is not given but is produced within certain modalities of power, discourses, and contexts.[51] While on stage during my competition, when I was complying with multiple gendered and other disciplinary regulations, my body had mattered. That is, my highly constructed body had been publicly revealed as matter, though not at all in the way that I had anticipated or planned for it to happen.

FIVE

Aftermath

The Photographs in My Purse

It has been ten months since my competition, and I am at a conference in Vancouver, British Columbia. A small group of academics and curators has met, exchanged chapter drafts destined for a forthcoming anthology on Canadian museums, and made brief public presentations. The hard work is done and we are enjoying a final banquet, relaxing and getting to know each other on a personal rather than strictly professional level. I reach into my purse and pull out a tattered brown envelope. Removing the glossy photographs inside, I reveal my secret past: I have competed in a bodybuilding/figure contest, taking to the stage in a tiny blue bikini. The reactions are mixed, ranging from shock to disbelief as the pictures are passed around the table. "Est-ce que c'est vraiment vous? [Is this really you?]" asks one scholar from Québec, finding little resemblance between the images and the fleshly being now seated across from her. "No, not really," I admit.

The built body primarily exists within the realm of photography. Bodybuilding and other fitness competitions are designed to produce still pictures of the ideally sculpted physiques of contestants, showing them at their peak. Many scholars who study bodybuilding have analyzed how these images both reinforce and undermine conventional understandings of gender, sexuality, class, and race.[1] Yet photographic practices inform all aspects of bodybuilding, from the early days of training to the precompetition months of strict dieting, even as they become more prominent during the contest itself, when every participant is photographed while on stage to create representations that can subsequently be displayed as signs of accomplishment. In this chapter I move beyond much previous literature by examining the multiple uses of photography in relation to bodybuilding, suggesting that diverse images can shift between categories to act as, among other things, documents, trophies, forms of self-promotion, and modes of forgetting.

What interests me most in this final chapter is the mobility of such imagery. Not only did prints of my staged photographs travel with me inside my purse, the digital versions were reproduced—and thereby recontextualized—in newspapers, selected bodybuilding magazines, and online. The meanings of these images changed continually, depending on the ways in which they were framed and the audiences interpreting them. In keeping with my consideration of the implications of immobility and movement throughout this book, the following discussion recognizes the apparent stillness of these pictures but concentrates on the seemingly endless transformation of their significance. My attention to transition positions the images as active, prompting me to consider the work that they do, as well as what they might mean to different groups. I argue that photographic technologies are themselves part of the performance of bodybuilding/figure identities. Fitness enthusiasts must participate in a series of photographic events in order to become (and to become recognized as) serious competitors.

This analysis necessarily engages with photographic theory, a vast literature dating from at least the nineteenth century. Recent publications have considered the relation between still images and film or video, challenging the idea that printed pictures are motionless.[2] Others have considered whether some photographs are speech acts that perform actions instead of exclusively describing events.[3] Many studies have highlighted the disciplinary aspects of photography, noting how photographic processes promote surveillance, transforming subjects into objects that can be traded, possessed, and evaluated.[4] While I allude to some of the debates in this field, I am primarily engaged with the research resulting from my autoethnographic Feminist Figure Girl project. Using my own experiences, I examine the roles of photography within the bodybuilding subculture, remarking on instances that either overlap with or diverge from the photographic conventions of other realms.

I begin the first section of this chapter by analyzing some of the pictures taken of and by me in 2010 when I attended the Olympia, an international bodybuilding competition held every September in Las Vegas, and end by considering the photographs made during my figure competition of June 2011. In addition to interpreting the site of representation, that is, the content and significance of the images in question, I study the site of reception, attending to how the pictures were understood by different consumers of them.[5] I include the most typical kinds of photography produced in relation to bodybuilding/figure contests, from the initial assessment images taken of me by my personal trainer to the weekly progress pictures that my partner quickly snapped and the staged images shot during the competition by David Ford, an established physique photographer. Even as I recognize the differences between these pictures, I argue that none of them simply stop time to freeze an image of the body, making it available for extended scrutiny. These inscriptions of my body are neither strictly indexical nor iconic—terms defined below—but invent another body that is never really present. At the same time, these images refer to the act of being photographed, an important collaborative event that establishes rather than merely records the identity of the bodybuilder/figure girl.

In the second section of this chapter, I turn to some of the alternative photographs of me produced by Patrick J. Reed, a visual artist and designer whom I hired immediately after he graduated with an MFA from the Department of Art and Design at the University of Alberta. Impressed with both Patrick's unorthodox pictures of American college girls participating in sorority culture and the pop art aesthetics of his printed works, I asked him to contribute to the Feminist Figure Girl project. Not only did Patrick work with another designer, Jeffrey Klassen, to create the FFG logo, produce special invitations to advertise my competition, and design T-shirts for my supporters to wear, he also unobtrusively photographed me while I trained, cooked food, and prepared for my show. Trusting in Patrick's skill and sensitivity, I did not dictate the process or outcome of his work, and the often striking results are due to his insight rather than to any sustained input from me. I argue that Patrick's photographs offer critical alternatives to the more standardized images discussed in part one. They focus on the hard work that was required to produce my body, showing my labor as dependent on a

community of supporters, both paid and unpaid. His pictures typically portray me in an unflattering light, grimacing, exhausted, and
stuffing food into an unwilling body. I pay special attention to the
images of me being painted with tanning dye by a friend the night
before my competition. In these pictures I am almost entirely naked,
pathetically vulnerable, and, at least in my opinion, desexualized. In
line with my emphasis on the performative potential of photography, I contend that these pictures are feminist interventions, offering
both an important counterpart to and critique of the standardized
images of figure girls.

Photographic Events

I first started thinking about the unique role of photography in bodybuilding while attending the 2010 Olympia with my friend and former trainer, Gillian Kovack. As an aspiring heavyweight bodybuilder
who plans to compete for the Ms. Olympia title in the future, Gill
was eager to "meet the athletes" at an event organized for this purpose the night before the competition. Bypassing the lines of fans
waiting to shake hands with Jay Cutler, then a three-time winner of
the Mr. Olympia title, we headed toward the relatively unpopulated
area in which the female bodybuilders were seated behind tables
laden with posters and photographs of them onstage. I was most
interested in meeting Iris Kyle, an American who had already won
the title of Ms. Olympia six times. Surprised by the lack of lineups,
we walked immediately up to Kyle, finding her looking understandably tired and bored. She nevertheless smiled and agreed to pose
for pictures with us (see feministfiguregirl.com). Kyle looked smaller
than I expected, based on the photographs of her that I had seen
in various muscle magazines. Dressed in a red outfit that concealed
most of her body, she made no attempt to impress fans by flexing or
posturing. Instead, we were directed to look at the officially staged
photos of Kyle that were for sale. In them, she appeared to be mas-
sive, with every striated muscle distinctively separated from the next.

At the time, I was struck by the apparent lack of connection
between the person standing beside me, and the images of Kyle

in her official photographs. It was clear that the staged pictures of
Kyle were not offered as inscriptions of an unchanging reality. Fans
were never invited to make links between the relaxed, clothed form
that they encountered at the "meet the athletes" event and Kyle's
staged physique as shown in her pictures. In semiotic terms, the
official photographs of Kyle as a bodybuilder were not framed as
iconic signs. According to the American semiotician Charles Sanders Peirce, iconic signs are based on the principle of resemblance
between the image and the thing it portrays.[6] In this representational mode, the image recognizably looks, sounds, feels, tastes, or
smells like the object it imitates. This conventional form of interpretation is often applied to the images of competitors in bodybuilding
magazines, which are assumed to represent the appearance of the
athletes. Indeed, I had performed such a reading by regarding published images of Kyle and then expecting to meet a visually similar
body "in the flesh" at the Olympia. Yet the principle of resemblance
was disrupted when I encountered Kyle at the "meet the athletes"
event. Her precompetition body was covered, not just to enhance the
effect of her corporeal revelation on stage the next day, but because it
was not the body that would finally appear. That posed body would
be different from the one that was currently present. It would be,
among other things, more dehydrated, shiny, and spot lit while striking a scripted set of muscular postures.

Nor were the photos displayed on Kyle's table offered as indexical signs. Peirce defines indexical signs as those based on a real con-
tiguity between the image and the object it purports to reproduce.[7]
A bullet hole, for example, could not have existed without the bullet
that made it, even if the bullet itself is no longer present. In this representational mode, the signifier (bullet hole) is caused by the sig-
nified (bullet). Various scholars have argued that photographs are
indexical signs produced by the inscription of light reflected from
a real object, or that photographic images have at least come to be
conventionally understood indexically as providing reliable evidence
of a real thing that exists or once existed in the world.[8] This commonplace approach to interpreting bodybuilding photographs—as
imprints of a body that previously appeared, however briefly—was
equally challenged by Kyle's relaxed presence at the "meet the athletes" event at the Olympia. The signifier (Kyle's built body) was not

caused by or attributable to Kyle's embodied being. Her built body was revealed as largely absent, appearing only within particular locations and by means of a specific set of conditions.

When I saw Kyle competing on stage the next day, she looked more like the impressive figure I had been anticipating. I obediently snapped a few pictures of her, resembling the ones that appear on her website (www.iriskyle.com). The memory of the exhausted and obliging form I had encountered the previous day nevertheless remained with me, encouraging me to think more critically about the photographic processes in which I was increasingly embedded. If the "meet the athletes" event had featured the absence of the built body, what then was the event's purpose? And why had I joined other fans by posing for photographs alongside my favored competitor? Why was I taking pictures of her on stage now? Glancing down at the inexpensive digital camera in my hand, I realized that the pre-competition and staged activities were fundamentally photographic events necessitating the involvement of fans as well as athletes. The pictures that I was taking of Kyle on stage were part of the production of both my identity and her built body. In other words, photography was a technology that did far more than record the results of bodybuilding; it was crucially involved in the collaborative production of bodybuilding.

Unlike the competition itself, the "meet the athletes" event had been staged for the construction and display of fans, not bodybuilders. By posing for a picture with Kyle, I was placed in a contiguous relationship with a professional bodybuilder, moving my own identity a little closer to hers, especially after I posted the resulting images on both Facebook and my blog site, feministfiguregirl.com. To a certain extent, the image of me standing beside Kyle, as well as the pictures I later snapped of her on stage, were offered to my friends and family members as iconic and indexical evidence of my presence at the Olympia, but they were also a requisite part of my socialization into the world of bodybuilding. According to literary critic Susan Sontag: "As photographs give people an imaginary possession of a past that is unreal, they also help people take possession of space in which they are insecure."[9] While Sontag alludes to the photographic practices related to tourism, her statement nevertheless sheds light on the way in which I was using photographic processes to appropriate the body of Kyle, attempting to possess it in a potentially aggressive manner, even as I took pictures in order to adopt a prescribed role and feel like less of an outsider while attending one of my first bodybuilding competitions. Kyle's identity as a bodybuilder was also dependent on this kind of power dynamic, though I found the particularities of it difficult to discern given her successful career and high profile. In contrast, my role as a novice to the practice of bodybuilding made it easier to see the simultaneously supportive and constraining aspects of photography. For even as I entered pre-established power dynamics I was willingly, perhaps inevitably, subject to them. I eventually realized that at the Olympia I had submitted to a number of photographic rituals that had allowed my gradual transition from bodybuilding fan to future figure competitor.

The photographic events I had experienced at the Olympia had done something that directly affected my identity. In keeping with my consideration of the Feminist Figure Girl project as a work of performance art in Chapter Four, I decided to approach the photographs related to and arising from my research as performative. Instead of following my usual method of undertaking a careful visual analysis of these pictures, highlighting the meanings conveyed by their content, form, composition, lighting, and allusion to other images, I would consider the work that they did. This approach was further informed by cultural critic Laura Levin's review of the expanding literature on photography and performance, which asks how images move beyond their frames to affect viewers.[10] Drawing on the arguments famously made by J. L. Austin in *How to Do Things with Words* (1962), Levin explains that just as performative utterances enact transformations, as when an minister says, "I now pronounce you husband and wife" to produce a marriage, so too can a photograph change the world rather than merely describing or recording it.[11] According to Levin, a performative reading of photography would focus on "the intersubjective relations that initiate the photograph's performative force and meaning."[12] In other words, someone analyzing photographs in this fashion would reinscribe dimensions of time and movement into the images, while attending to their reception. I nevertheless wanted to go a little further, by additionally focusing on the intersubjective relations that had produced the photograph in the first place, considering the act of making it as another form of creative labor with tangible results.

I did not become a future figure competitor until October 18, 2010. That is when I entered a small, dimly lit consultation room with my current personal trainer, Audrey Shepherd, and removed my workout pants and T-shirt to reveal a pink 1950s bathing suit. Standing awkwardly against a cold wall, I handed Audrey my camera, and she took pictures of me from the front, back, and both sides. I did not flex, pose, or try to suck in my gut. I was not tanned or wearing makeup, and my hair was not done. The resulting pictures are hardly flattering, and lack any contextual markers, except for the weight scale beside me, a potentially ironic allusion to the fat-loss diet program I would start three months later. Although this photographic event was in many ways banal, it conferred my identity as someone in training for a bodybuilding/figure competition. I was transformed by disrobing and posing as a body both deserving of and desiring scrutiny. This photographic act was also a disciplinary exercise that positioned me as an object waiting to be compared and contrasted with other bodies, recalling art historian John Tagg's arguments about nineteenth-century photography as a state apparatus that participated in producing regimes of truth able to hold citizens in place.[13] By submitting to these "before" photographs, I had opened my body to the application of rules and regulations, while requiring viewers to look at me in a judgmental way. At the same time, the pictures were made within an atmosphere of trust, initially viewed only by myself and Audrey, creating an intimate bond between us. I reproduce one of the images below as a material representation rather than a document of that transformative occurrence.

I later had occasion to participate in a similarly transformative event, albeit from the position of the one taking the photographs rather than as the body on display. In December of 2013 a friend decided to enter a figure contest, the same entry level in which I had competed a year and a half earlier. Portraying her decision as a kind of midlife crisis, she was primarily in pursuit of the photographs that would be taken of her on stage. "When I am older," she asserted, "I want to show my kids what I looked like at age 40." In this case, my friend understood photography as an indexical practice able to record the truth of her appearance. Yet she strikingly located her body as always elsewhere, looking to the future to create a body that would exist in the past. Even as her goals differed from mine, she began by submitting to the same process as I had done, posing for

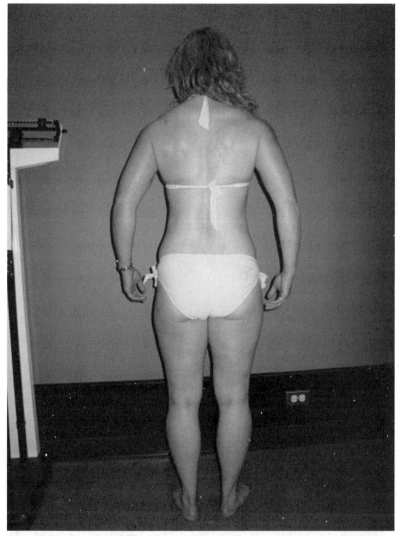

Figure 5.1. Lianne McTavish in the "before" photograph taken by Audrey Shepherd in October 2010 (courtesy of Lianne McTavish).

"before" shots at the gym to create pictures that would be viewed by a select group of trusted friends and professional trainers. Her commitment to the competition was primarily enacted by means of the production of these pictures, and not by the appearance or content of the images themselves.

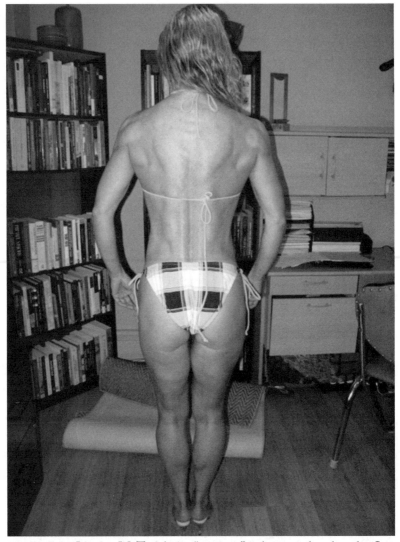

Figure 5.2. Lianne McTavish in "progress"; photograph taken by Lee Spence in April 2011 (courtesy of Lianne McTavish).

Once I started my precompetition diet in January 2011, I posed for weekly progress photos that were e-mailed to my diet coach, Raejha Douziech. In this case, I donned a smaller string bikini to reveal more of my body, especially the problem glute area, and wore my four-inch-high posing shoes. Following Raejha's instructions, I struck the same four quarter poses every Friday morning after emptying my bladder but before eating or showering. Raejha would compare the pictures with those of the previous week, making judgments before sending me an altered diet program. In this case, Raejha understood the photographs as documents that provided evidence of my physical condition. I was struck, however, by the fact that she preferred to work from images rather than see me in person, something she did regularly during our posing sessions together at her studio. Raejha claimed she could observe my body changing more easily in the two-dimensional format, and furthermore needed to place the dated images of me side by side on her computer screen for comparative purposes. Recalling Eleanor Antin's photographic installation, *Carving: A Traditional Sculpture* (1972), in which the artist documented her weight loss, as discussed in Chapter Four, my weekly progress photos were not considered transparent; they mediated my body to produce a discernibly different and more legible version of it, containing references to change over time within their apparent stillness.

I myself barely looked at these weekly images, and did not bother to save many of them. My role was to submit to this photographic event and negotiate the power dynamics that it encouraged. This repeated practice was indeed disciplinary, as it required me to show tangible signs of "improvement" by stringently following my diet to achieve a progressively leaner physique. These photographs established my compliance with Raejha's program. At the same time, they required the participation of my partner, who quickly snapped the pictures of me before rushing off to work every Friday morning. This process forced him to play a role in a project that he did not fully support, even as it revealed my continued reliance on him, and many others, in order to proceed.

The next disciplinary exercise that involved photography was the most public one, involving my presentation onstage during the competition itself. The pictures of me wearing tanning dye, a blue velvet bikini, posing shoes, full makeup, and hair extensions are arguably the most flattering ones, taken under ideal conditions by the highly skilled physique photographer David Ford. They are also by far the most reproduced images stemming from the Feminist Figure Girl project. Yet in my opinion these particular photographs convey the least amount of information about my research.

As indicated in Chapter Four, my on-stage experience was painful and unpleasant, aspects that are erased from the resulting pictures. To my eyes, these images are primarily about absence, for they lack any tangible link to either the goals of, or the labor involved in, my extensive preparations. Nor do these photographs reveal the reality of my poor performance on stage. I nevertheless carry these particular images in my purse as a form of documentation that is not based on iconic or indexical principles. For me, these pictures do not show viewers what I had looked like. Instead they are akin to a graduation diploma, driver's license, or passport, supplying official proof of an identity that was both achieved and can be recognized by means of established regulations.[14]

These staged photographs have produced, however, a wide range of responses from the diverse viewers who have subsequently encountered them. When I gave academic lectures about my work in the months following the competition, certain members of the audience expressed admiration at the "courageous risk" I had taken by potentially undermining my authority and opening myself to criticism.[15] In the previous chapter, I have already considered and then discounted this assessment by reflecting on my privileged position as a full professor. Others attending these lectures contrastingly looked on my staged photos as a form of compliance rather than a challenge. One feminist scholar demanded to know why my pictures were gaining national attention when her own projects were consistently overlooked by the media, suggesting that my bikini-clad body was distracting attention away from truly feminist issues of more pressing concern.[16] Her comments prompted me to consider further the political ramifications of my project, particularly whether I had engaged in a form of postfeminism, a subject I addressed in Chapter Three of this book. At the same time, more than a few of the women in the audience perceived my photographs as judgments directed at their own bodies and lifestyles. One young student exclaimed, "But it has taken me a long time to learn to love my fat ass!"[17] At first I was unsure how to respond, bewildered by the idea that my staged pictures had anything to do with her buttocks. Then I realized she was interpreting the photos of me onstage according to the conventions of advertising, seeing them as the "after" images typically included in promotions for diet programs. By viewing my images as arguments in favor of weight loss, she was interpolated as a fat person in need of reform.

The different responses to my onstage photographs continued to multiply once the images appeared in national newspapers,
on line, and in a few bodybuilding magazines. I have already discussed some of the most negative responses in Chapter Four, which
stemmed from a small group of conservative men who considered
me hideous, sterile, and monstrous. A few of those viewers went further by offering me some corrective advice about how to improve my
appearance. In this case, they had applied the conventions of porno-
graphic imagery to my pictures and subsequently found my appearance sadly lacking. One member of the "men's rights" forum in
question helpfully posted a picture of what he considered a truly sexy
woman equipped with what he called "natural feminine beauty." The
image showed a young, soft woman smiling compliantly while bending over to display her large breast implants and surgically enhanced
buttocks.[18] While his intervention was clearly misogynistic and can
perhaps be easily dismissed, it provides additional evidence of the
mobility of my staged photographs, both in terms of the locations
in which they appeared and the interpretive conventions that were
applied to them. The multiple meanings gleaned from my staged
photographs had little to do with me and continue to proliferate
beyond my control.

The openness of these photographs should nevertheless be perceived as a positive rather than negative trait. The images are clearly
not static, offering singular or obvious messages. They are therefore
available for reconfiguration, a process that I can encourage rather
than attempt to curtail. Perhaps I can shape a distinctive vision of
my project and of bodybuilding/figure competitions more generally
by participating in the creation of alternative photographs, something considered below. In the second half of this chapter, I challenge the staged images of me, which erase references to time and
labor, by supplementing them with other photographs that are not
more accurate per se but do different kinds of work.

Photographic Disruptions

Three months before the competition, Patrick headed to my gym to
photograph one of my weight-training sessions with Audrey. "After
the first few minutes, you won't even know I'm there," he promised.

He was right. A consummate professional, Patrick knew exactly how to make himself practically invisible, working around the awkward space of the commercial gym to capture the interactions between me and my personal trainer. Our photo shoot was, however, far from spontaneous. It had been planned months beforehand because I needed to acquire written permission from the fitness manager, who generously agreed to support my research on the condition that we shoot only when the gym was least busy and not interfere with any patrons who might be present. The application for ethical clearance from my university was more arduous, involving a lengthy application process that had obviously been designed to protect vulnerable individuals from potentially harmful medical and scientific research. Once the ethics committee finally agreed that our photographic practices would not exploit anyone at the gym, we moved ahead with them. In striking contrast to my earlier interaction with photography at the Olympia and in the private consultation room, the photo shoots at the gym were immediately positioned within the realm of power dynamics, understood as activities that did not merely record given events, but produced new knowledge that could affect people's identities.

Many of the resulting photographs portray the construction of my figure girl body as an arduous procedure involving ongoing collaboration and care. In one striking image, Audrey stands behind me as I perform lat pull-downs—the latissimus dorsi muscles of figure girls are ideally wide, helping to accentuate a small waist. My personal trainer is shown in a supporting role, positioned as a key figure overseeing my controlled activities. In contrast to her attentive looking at my back muscles, the bar of the weight machine covers my eyes. This particular pose suggests my intense focus on the exercise undertaken rather than on the world around me. My looking has been replaced by that of Audrey, reinforcing the idea that we are working together to shape a new image of my body. Patrick takes the place of the viewer, standing apart from the central dyad yet close enough to frame the scene tightly, a decision that enhances the intimacy of the pair absorbed in work, while highlighting the constraining exercise technologies that hold me in place, isolating my back muscles. The resulting image breaks from conventional training pictorials, which often show such bodybuilders as Iris Kyle alone, working toward a distant goal with little encouragement.

Figure 5.3. Patrick J. Reed photograph of Lianne McTavish training with Audrey Shepherd in March 2011 (courtesy of Lianne McTavish).

Another commonplace depiction of working out in gyms features group dynamics; consider the film *Pumping Iron II*, which portrays heavyweight bodybuilder Bev Francis being treated like "one of the boys" by her male coach as he loudly demands that she lift heavier and push out more reps.[19] In contrast to these representations of intensive action, the photograph produced by Patrick offers a vision of training as a quiet, caring, and methodical practice based on mutual trust.

The photograph is as much about touching as it is about looking, drawing attention to the embodied nature of training. Another view of the same gym session reveals that Audrey is pressing down on my trapezius muscles to immobilize them. My disproportionately large upper back was at odds with the ideally smaller figure girl form, and my goal was to shrink my traps in time for the show. When my diet coach, Raejha, first saw me in her studio, she asked, "So are you a bodybuilder or are you a figure girl?" in part because of my oversized trapezius muscles. This growth was not caused by heavy shoulder shrugs—an exercise I never performed—but by my tendency to hold tension continually in my upper back and shoulders. Despite Audrey's helpful interventions, my large traps remained a problem, and I attempted to hide this defect on stage by wearing my long hair down to cover them. In any case, the image below reinforces my reliance on Audrey's assistance, confirming that my musculature was not entirely under my own control. To my mind, both photos intervene in typical images of bodybuilders and figure girls by insisting that the process of competing involves both recognizing and compensating for weaknesses. The pictures offer helpful correctives to the commonsense assumption that participating in such contests primarily requires the successful domination of unruly flesh.

About a month later, Patrick accompanied me to a posing session with Raejha, having received her permission to photograph us together in her studio. The resulting images again portray my trust in and reliance on experts, while also showing the tedious kind of labor involved in preparing for a bodybuilding/figure competition, unknown to most outsiders, and invisible in the more overtly posed pictures on stage. I contend that the following two photographs are active interventions for two reasons. First, they represent my awkward efforts to resemble another body and strike poses that are in no way natural. They depict me as a novice, actively engaged in learning from someone with more experience as I struggle to enact a new role. Second, the pictures feature references to place, including such details as boxes and plants. Portrayed as anything but glamorous, my precompetition regime is firmly situated within the world of everyday labor, shown as comparable to mundane office work.

Figure 5.4. Patrick J. Reed photograph of Lianne McTavish training with Audrey Shepherd in March 2011 (courtesy of Lianne McTavish).

In a later photo shoot, Patrick joined me in my own condo as I prepared meals by cooking and weighing precise amounts of food, something I did on an almost daily basis. The images produced show the domestic labor of competing, highlighting the routine chores that getting on stage necessitates. More important, the pictures associate the appearance of my flesh with the consumption of particular kinds of food. I find especially effective the representation of my truncated arm hovering over a stovetop complete with pots of cooking Brussels sprouts, asparagus, and a tray of roasted sweet potatoes. The vascularity (prominent veins) in my arm, enhanced by the low level of subcutaneous fat in my body, is shown in a contiguous relationship with the fibrous vegetables, drawing an association of causality between them. This suggestion of the interior workings of my body is enhanced by Patrick's close-up shot of bubbling chicken breasts, which I ate daily during the entire five months of my precompetition diet. Their shiny materiality alludes to the visceral nature of my own anatomy, which is becoming ever more visible as my fat stores decrease. Patrick's image of the chicken that I ingested further recalls the abject images of vomit and waste produced by contemporary artist Cindy Sherman, including her *Untitled #175*,

Figure 5.5. Patrick J. Reed photograph of Lianne McTavish posing with Raejha Douziech in May 2011 (courtesy of Lianne McTavish).

from 1987.[20] According to theorist Julia Kristeva, abject substances, often linked with maternity, fluidity, and digestion, are rejected as disgusting in order to create and maintain the illusion of a bounded, independent subject.[21] Disruptive associations nevertheless remain with that which is cast off. The troubling status of what lies inside, fueling my lean and muscular body, is invoked by the tight shot of monochromatic, slippery chicken flesh.

Figure 5.6. Patrick J. Reed photograph of Lianne McTavish posing with Raejha Douziech in May 2011 (courtesy of Lianne McTavish).

The days preceding my competition were packed with increasingly exhausting preparations, including dehydration and fat-loading rituals. Patrick continued to portray both the banal aspects and embodied nature of these experiences, including one striking image of me sewing snaps into my posing suit the night before my show. Although I had selected and ordered my suit months earlier, it arrived at the last minute, delayed by American customs agents

Figure 5.7. Patrick J. Reed photograph of Lianne McTavish preparing her diet food in April 2011 (courtesy of Lianne McTavish).

Figure 5.8. Patrick J. Reed photograph of Lianne McTavish's diet food (chicken) in April 2011 (courtesy of Lianne McTavish).

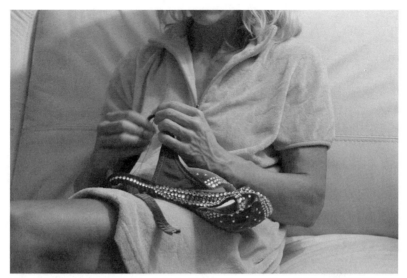

Figure 5.9. Patrick J. Patrick J. Reed photograph of Lianne McTavish sewing her posing suit in June 2011 (courtesy of Lianne McTavish).

and an impending strike by Canada Post. I was forced to draw on my minimal sewing talents to alter it on my own. The photograph produced by Patrick shows me seated on my couch, wearing a hideous pink housedress to protect my furnishings from the tanning dye applied to my body. My vascular hands, resembling those of an elderly woman, struggle with the needle and thread. The dowdy and aged figure portrayed in this image contrasts with the expensive crystal-encrusted bikini that I am in the process of fashioning. By condensing and thwarting the typical before and after pictures, this photograph indicates that attire is among the most important elements of posing as a figure girl.

In my opinion, arguably the most feminist images formed from my research were of me being "painted," that is, slathered in tanning dye the night before my competition. My former trainer and friend Gill assisted me with the process, just as I had helped her prepare for her own show more than a year earlier. The messy application of dark body paint took place in a small bathroom in my condo, forcing Patrick to perch inside the bathtub to achieve the various shots of Gill and me at work. I hesitated before including these photos in the

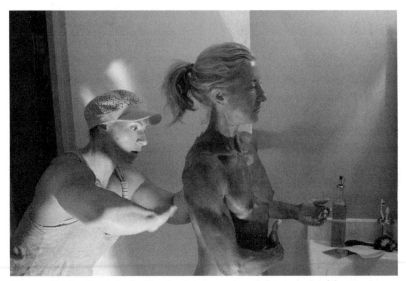

Figure 5.10. Patrick J. Reed photograph of Lianne McTavish being painted with tanning dye by Gillian Kovack in June 2011 (courtesy of Lianne McTavish).

book, for I am practically naked in them, wearing only a small pink thong. I feared viewers might sexualize these images, or cast judgment on them, responses at odds with my view of them as portraying scenes of feminist community and support. In the end, however, I decided to include what are for me touching scenes of vulnerability and exposure, realizing that I cannot hope to control the interpretation of these or other images stemming from my project. My decision to publish these photographs was influenced by the visit of Heather Cassils to the University of Alberta in November of 2012, as discussed in Chapter Four. The way in which this artist used the body to send open-ended messages was inspiring, as was the published article relating to Cassils's attempts to intervene in the exploitation of nude models by artist Vanessa Beecroft. Cassils's efforts to undermine Beecroft's practices from within, by working for her, were ultimately frustrated by the economic and institutional dynamics of the situation.[22] I decided to risk a similar frustration by releasing these photos, hoping they will be viewed within a long tradition of feminist efforts to reclaim and recode gendered flesh.[23]

Figure 5.11. Patrick J. Reed photograph of Lianne McTavish being painted with tanning dye the night before her competition by Gillian Kovack in June 2011 (courtesy of Lianne McTavish).

Figure 5.12. Patrick J. Reed photograph of Lianne McTavish being painted with tanning dye by Gillian Kovack in June 2011 (courtesy of Lianne McTavish).

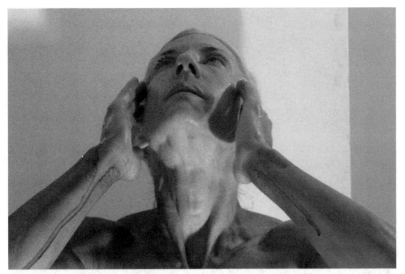

Figure 5.13. Patrick J. Reed photograph of Lianne McTavish covered in tanning dye in June 2011 (courtesy of Lianne McTavish).

After retouching my tan the morning of the show, I headed off to the hair salon, followed by a visit to the makeup studio. Patrick was with me during this entire process, taking photographs that depicted what I considered my increasing objectification as I moved ever closer to the stage. These selected images highlight the application of technology to my body, reconfirming that my appearance was meticulously crafted as part of a group effort. I chose to include the photo of me eating for the way in which it conveys the ugly aspects of precompetition rituals, particularly those immediately preceding walking on stage. In this image, I am exhausted while shoving meat into an unwilling body and enduring the lengthy application of heavy hair extensions. The accompanying photograph was taken as a professional stylist applied yet another set of implements designed to reshape my body, rendering it "stage ready."

I conclude this series of photographic interventions with a single shot of me on stage. By far the best pictures taken by Patrick during the event itself position me as one among many other competitors, jockeying for space under hot spotlights. However, for ethical reasons I cannot reproduce those group photos here, so I am including only one version of me walking awkwardly across the stage in

Figure 5.14. Patrick J. Reed photograph of Lianne McTavish eating cold steak while having her hair done by Toccara Winterhawk on the morning of her figure competition in June 2011 (courtesy of Lianne McTavish).

Figure 5.15. Patrick J. Reed photograph of Lianne McTavish having her makeup professionally applied on the morning of her figure competition in June 2011 (courtesy of Lianne McTavish).

Figure 5.16. Patrick J. Reed photograph of Lianne McTavish exiting the stage during her figure competition in June 2011 (courtesy of Lianne McTavish).

a rather unladylike fashion. I selected this image for its portrayal of how my constructed body ultimately did not overcome either my personal physical limitations or the weight of my material body in order to play the ideal role of a gracefully fit and feminine flirt. To my mind, this picture epitomizes my experience of wanting to exit the stage as quickly as possible, but, in keeping with my minimal framing of the images above, I will not attempt a detailed interpretation, thus respecting the mutliple possible readings that viewers might formulate.

Conclusions

Patrick J. Reed's photographic interventions provide a response and critique of the images usually reproduced to represent my project in newspapers and magazines. In keeping with standardized images of figure girls and bodybuilders, those typically selected by members of the media show a polished and confident individual posing with tensed muscles while standing triumphantly alone on stage. Such images enable forgetting, effectively both erasing and displacing the hard and often tedious labor that spectacularized the body on display.[24] The photographs included in the second section of this chapter are by no means more accurate or less staged than the conventional ones. Yet they have been constructed to highlight the unattractive aspects of competing, including the domestic and often mundane hard work that went into my transformation from professor to figure girl. Patrick's images furthermore focus on the communal production of this body, undermining the assumption that competing is an individual achievement. His pictures portray a body that is dependent on others; it is enfleshed, tired, sore, and ultimately uncontrollable. It can also be abject, uncomfortable, and unappealing to regard. In the end, these photographs both accept and offer the built body as a site where meanings are made, opening this body's potential to convey such feminist values as mutual care and the pursuit of sustained thought.

A primary goal of this chapter was to avoid viewing photographs as passive inscriptions of events and activate them by considering the work that they do. In the first section, I did so by emphasizing the performative nature of the photographic process in my transition from bodybuilding enthusiast to future figure competitor. I finally became recognizable as a figure girl once I submitted to a set of disciplinary photographic conventions, including the "before" shots taken by Audrey and the weekly progress photos that allowed my physique to come into being as an object for scrutiny. Even as the second section of this chapter examined the regulated and collaborative nature of the photographs taken by Patrick, it centered more on the site of representation—that is, on their actual content. I adopted this approach because the subject matter of these pictures is relatively novel, at odds with the usual depictions of figure girls. I also wanted to resist any effort to control their meanings, ensuring they would remain open to different audiences. Participating in and thinking about photography helped me to learn that becoming a figure girl necessitates giving oneself over to a range of technologies, accepting a lack of control over the process as well as the results.

Afterword

"Would numbers 11, 12, 13, and 14 come to the front of the stage, please? Now hit your front pose, ladies. Make one quarter-turn to the side. And now to the back." As I tense my muscles and flare my lats, I reach up to sweep my heavy dyed blonde hair off my shoulders, employing a flourishing gesture that I have practiced over a hundred times. Suddenly the entire crowd lets out an audible gasp. My bra has fallen off, accidentally unhooked by the long gel nails recently welded to my hands. With lightening reflexes, I grab the front of my chest while clumsily attempting to rehook the clasp behind my neck. I cannot manage it. The announcer eventually calls an assistant to the stage, and she remedies the situation. I never stop smiling throughout the ordeal. After all, it is in many ways the perfect culmination of my Feminist Figure Girl research project.

The story of my "wardrobe malfunction" encapsulates the main themes of this book, including references to vision, display, intervention, embodied experience, performance, posing, collaboration, audience feedback, and, most of all, the kind of failure that is enabling. The public revelation of my shrunken, dieted breasts was by no means planned. I need to confirm the fortuitous nature of this event because about a week before the show I had announced my desire to act subversively while on stage. Inspired by tales of feminist interventions at beauty pageants during the 1960s, I had threatened to shout empowering slogans while posing or else bend over to moon the judges. Yet when the day of the contest finally arrived, I was simply too tired to resist the competition's script in a deliberate fashion. Luckily, it all worked out in the end.

In keeping with my training in visual culture, this project was designed to turn me into a spectacle. Evidence of my art historical knowledge weaves throughout the book, perhaps most prominently in Chapter One, which contrasts the overt scrutiny of objectified muscles involved in bodybuilding with both the strictly numerical evaluation of participants at Weight Watchers meetings and the interiorized vision of physicality encouraged during hatha yoga sessions. I was continually struck, however, by what was typically not shown, and what was intentionally hidden, in most accounts of bodybuilding. In Chapter Five I strove to reveal the mundane and repetitive labor of preparing to compete, including photographs of me working out, cooking chicken, learning to pose, and being slathered in tanning dye. My goal was not to represent the "truth" of figure or bodybuilding contests but to offer an alternative vision of them, one that was far from glamorous. I additionally wished to include an image of me standing topless on stage, causing mayhem. Unfortunately no such picture exists. Patrick was so startled by the incident that he neglected to capture it. When I turned to the videotaped version of the event, available for purchase from the sponsoring Alberta Bodybuilding Association, I discovered that my interruption had been excised from the recording. This visual absence serves to highlight the careful construction and staging of the built body, while indicating how challenging it is to resist the disciplinary mechanisms that produce it.

Despite my attention to vision, for the most part I stepped out of my comfort zone during this research project by refusing to undertake the formal analysis and visual comparison of aesthetic objects. In an effort to think and work differently, I focused on embodiment, leading me to attend to touch and other senses. I wanted to convey, for instance, what it felt like to lift weights, arguing in Chapter Two that muscle failure had disrupted my body schema, opening new learning opportunities for me. My discussion of the enabling effects of physical stillness took issue with the often unreflective preference for movement in much of the feminist scholarship informed by phenomenology. I continued this thread in my fourth chapter by drawing on the inspirational work of artists Marina Abramović and Heather Cassils to shed light on the hard labor of remaining motionless. All the same, my efforts to valorize the stillness of posing did not rest on a concurrent denigration of movement. In keeping with Maurice Merleau-Ponty's association of physical engagement with meaningful expression, my research project had been instigated by my increasing activity at the gym, as I lifted heavier weights and was overwhelmed by endorphin rushes during intensive cardio workouts. The importance of movement returned most strongly in my final chapter, in which I approached photography as an active event that "does" something, insisting that aspiring competitors must submit to specific photographic practices, including the production of "before" pictures, to establish their identities. The actual content of these pictures is of secondary importance at best.

Overall, I wished to intervene in feminist scholarship and accounts of fitness culture by offering a novel version of bodybuilding and figure practices. Instead of assuming that this physique culture involved aggressive posturing designed to control the body and inflate narcissistic egos, I found that pursuing a built body necessitated accepting a lack of physical control within the nurturing circle of care created by trainers, coaches, and friends. I consider my accounts of this experience to promote feminist values without being prescriptive or creating new rules for pursuing health, fitness, and community. To this end, I grounded most discussions in the particularities of my position as a privileged professor, interacting in identifiable places with specific people. The scenes of my experience took place in corporate gyms, private consultation rooms, the perimeter around an abortion clinic in Fredericton, and backstage at an entry-level figure competition in Edmonton. These encounters were created by means of constant collaboration, as I worked with personal trainers, diet coaches, skilled designers, professional photographers, and fellow figure contestants to make this project a reality. My dependence on others, and their generous willingness to help me, was by far the most rewarding—and I would argue the most feminist—aspect of the knowledge produced from the Feminist Figure Girl endeavor.

As indicated in the Introduction, I had initially feared that by taking up an autoethnographic approach, my work would be either descriptive or self-indulgent or both. In my opinion, these fears were rarely realized. The collaborative nature of this research extended beyond the group directly assisting me to include my work colleagues, the readers of my blog, and a broad public that responded both positively and negatively to the media accounts of my research. Instead of directing undue attention toward myself, the autoethnographic method allowed me to engage with others openly. The final form of this book was shaped in large part by the questions people asked me, often in challenging ways, about the actual feminist content of Feminist Figure Girl, and whether my process had anything in common with a work of durational performance art. In striving to answer their queries, I was led to consider what were for me new theoretical approaches to the body, including those stemming from phenomenology, and ultimately contribute to the debates surrounding such issues as the definition of postfeminism, vagaries of place, and political possibilities of performance. An autoethnographic framework furthermore allowed me to take risks, making a public display of my precompetition diet before standing on a stage while wearing a bikini and other ultrafeminine accoutrements. This risk-taking paid off in my literal failure to enact the role of a figure girl, demonstrating, among other things, Judith Butler's contention that gender is a series of reiterated performances that are never really achieved but that also cannot simply be chosen at will.

One final question that is almost always posed by those learning about my project is, "Will you ever compete again?" In this case, my answer is a firm no, for I do not believe that I would learn anything new from this particular repetition. Now that the project is over, I will no doubt conceive of another one that is completely different, though its parameters have not yet occurred to me. Based on the outcome of Feminist Figure Girl I can, however, rest assured that more failure is definitely in my future.

Notes

Introduction

1. Stacy Holman Jones, "Autoethnography: Making the Personal Political," in *The Sage Handbook of Qualitative Research*, 3rd ed., eds. Norman K. Denzin and Yvonna S. Lincoln (Thousand Oaks, CA: Sage, 2005), 766.

2. Lianne McTavish, "The Cultural Production of Pregnancy: Bodies and Embodiment at a New Brunswick Abortion Clinic," *Topia: Canadian Journal of Cultural Studies* 20 (Fall 2008): 23–42.

3. See, for example, Douglas Sadao Aoki, "Posing the Subject: Sex, Illumination, and *Pumping Iron II: The Women*," *Cinema Journal* 4 (Summer 1999): 24–44, and Anne Balsamo, "Feminist Bodybuilding," *Technologies of the Gendered Body: Reading Cyborg Women* (Durham, NC: Duke University Press, 1996), 41–55.

4. Barbara Brook, *Feminist Perspectives on the Body* (London: Longman, 1999), 118–22, and Chris Holmlund, "Visible Difference and Flex Appeal: The Body, Sex, Sexuality, and Race in the *Pumping Iron* Films," in *Building Bodies*, ed. Pamela L. Moore (New Brunswick, NJ: Rutgers University Press, 1997), 87–102.

5. Pamela L. Moore, "Feminist Bodybuilding, Sex, and the Interruption of Investigative Knowledge," in *Building Bodies*, 74–86.

6. Lianne McTavish, *Childbirth and the Display of Authority in Early Modern France* (Aldershot: Ashgate, 2005).

7. R. Danielle Egan, Katherine Frank, and Merri Lisa Johnson,

eds., *Flesh for Fantasy: Producing and Consuming Exotic Dance* (New York: Thunder's Mouth Press, 2006), Carolyn Ellis, *The Ethnographic I: A Methodological Novel about Autoethnography* (Walnut Creek, CA: Altamira, 2004), Paula Saukko, *The Anorexic Self: A Personal, Political Analysis of Diagnostic Discourse* (Albany, NY: State University of New York Press, 2008), Lisa M. Tillmann-Healy, "A Secret Life in a Culture of Thinness: Reflections on Body, Food, and Bulimia," in *Composing Ethnography: Alternative Forms of Qualitative Writing*, eds. C. Ellis and A. P. Bochner (Walnut Creek, CA: Altamira Press, 1996), 76–108, and Lisa M. Tillmann, "Body and Bulimia Revisited: Reflections on 'A Secret Life'," *Journal of Applied Communication Research* 37, 1 (February 2009): 98–112.

8. Tillmann-Healy, "A Secret Life in a Culture of Thinness," 77.

9. Heewon Chang, *Autoethnography as Method* (Walnut Creek, CA: Altamira Press, 2008), 9.

10. Ellis, *The Ethnographic I*, xix.

11. Jacquelyn Allen Collinson and John Hockey, "Autoethnography: Self-indulgence or Rigorous Methodology?" *Philosophy and the Sciences of Exercise, Health and Sport: Critical Perspectives on Research Methods* (New York: Routledge, 2005), 193.

12. See, for example, Tanya Bunsell, *Strong and Hard Women: An Ethnography of Female Bodybuilding* (London: Routledge, 2013).

13. See, for example, Samuel Wilson Fussell, *Muscle: Confessions of an Unlikely Bodybuilder* (New York: Perennial, 1991).

14. Collinson and Hockey, "Autoethnography: Self-indulgence or Rigorous Methodology?" 187–202.

15. See Andrew C. Sparkes, "Autoethnography," *Telling Tales in Sport and Physical Activity: A Qualitative Journey* (Champaign, IL: Human Kinetics, 2002), 73–105, and Holman Jones, "Autoethnography: Making the Personal Political," 783–84.

16. Chang, *Autoethnography as Method*, 13.

17. My understanding of subjectivity stems primarily from a graduate course I took with Kaja Silverman at the University of Rochester. See Kaja Silverman, *Male Subjectivity at the Margins* (New York: Routledge, 1992). My discussion of experience was inspired by a talk given by Aron Vinegar. See his *I am a Monument: On Learning from Las Vegas* (Cambridge, MA: MIT Press, 2008).

18. Cited in Homan Jones, "Autoethnography: Making the Personal Political," 765.

19. See Ellis, *The Ethnographic I.* Chang, *Autoethnography as Method*, 54, warns against an excessive reliance on memory as a data source.

20. Cited in Holman Jones, "Autoethnography: Making the Personal Political," 7.

21. Niall Richardson, "Flex-rated! Female Bodybuilding: Feminist Resistance or Erotic Spectacle?" *Journal of Gender Studies* 17, 4 (December 2008): 292.

22. Judith Butler, *Gender Trouble: Feminism and the Subversion of Identity* (New York: Routledge, 1999).

23. See, for example, Eugene Y. Wang, "Watching the Steps: Peripatetic Vision in Medieval China," in *Visuality Before and Beyond the Renaissance: Seeing as Others Saw*, ed. Robert S. Nelson (Cambridge: Cambridge University Press, 1997), 116–42, Jonathan Crary, *Techniques of the Observer: On Vision and Modernity in the Nineteenth Century* (Cambridge, MA: MIT Press, 1990), and Lianne McTavish, "Learning to See in New Brunswick, 1862–1929," *Canadian Historical Review* 87, 4 (December 2006): 553–81.

24. Cressida J. Heyes, "Foucault Goes to Weight Watchers," *Hypatia* 21, 2 (Spring 2006): 126–49.

25. Dorothea Olkowski and Gail Weiss, eds., *Feminist Interpretations of Maurice Merleau-Ponty* (University Park, PA: The Pennsylvania State University Press, 2006).

26. Simone de Beauvoir and Iris Marion Young, *On Female Body Experience: "Throwing Like a Girl" and Other Essays* (New York: Oxford University Press, 2005).

27. Fussell, *Muscle: Confessions of an Unlikely Bodybuilder.* See also Alan M. Klein, *Little Big Men: Bodybuilding Subculture and Gender Construction* (Albany, NY: State University Press of New York, 1993).

28. Michel Foucault, *The History of Sexuality: An Introduction*, trans. Robert Hurley (New York: Vintage Books, 1990), 157. See also Pirkko Markula, *Foucault, Sport and Exercise: Power, Knowledge and Transforming the Self* (Abingdon: Routledge, 2006), and Simon Crossley, "In the Gym: Motives, Meaning and Moral Careers," *Body and Society* 12 (June 2006), 23–50.

Chapter One. Measuring Up

1. Michel Foucault, *Discipline and Punish: The Birth of the Prison,* trans. Alan Sheridan (New York: Vintage, 1979).
2. Michel Foucault, "Governmentality," trans. Rosi Braidotti in *The Foucault Effect: Studies in Governmentality,* eds. Graham Burchell, Colin Gordon, and Peter Miller (Chicago, IL: University of Chicago Press, 1991), 87–104. Briefly, governmentality can be defined as the way governments and others attempt to produce citizens best suited to fulfill those governments' policies, and the organized practices (mentalities, rationalities, and techniques) through which subjects are governed.
3. Brian Pronger, *Body Fascism: Salvation in the Technology of Physical Fitness* (Toronto: University of Toronto Press, 1992). See also Pirkko Markula, *Foucault, Sport and Exercise: Power, Knowledge and Transforming the Self* (New York: Routledge, 2006).
4. Michel Foucault, *Introduction to the History of Sexuality,* vol. 1, trans. Robert Hurley (New York: Vintage, 1990), 95.
5. This particular part of my research, entitled "Feminist Figure Girl: Comparison," received ethics approval from the REB at the University of Alberta (Pro00019415).
6. I discuss autoethnography and provide some examples of the methodology in the Introduction to this book.
7. See, for example, Alan M. Klein, *Little Big Men: Bodybuilding Subculture and Gender Construction* (New York: SUNY Press, 1993), Maria Lowe, *Women of Steel: Female Bodybuilders and the Struggle for Self-Definition* (New York: New York University Press, 1998), Pamela L. Moore, *Building Bodies* (Newark, NJ: Rutgers University Press, 1997), and Camilla Obel, "Collapsing Gender in Competitive Bodybuilding: Researching Contradiction and Ambiguity in Sport," in *Gender and Sport: A Reader,* eds. Sheila Scraton and Anne Flintoff (London: Routledge, 2002), 241–54.
8. *Women's Health* magazine (March 2010): 132.
9. Karen Sessions, *Figure Competition Secrets* (Karen Sessions Inc., 2010) (http://www.figurecompetitionsecrets.com/?hop=index40).
10. Elwood Watson and Darcy Martin, eds., *"There She Is, Miss America": The Politics of Sex, Beauty, and Race in America's Most*

Famous Pageant (New York: Palgrave MacMillan, 2004), and Sarah Banet-Weiser, *The Most Beautiful Girl in the World: Beauty Pageants and National Identity* (Berkeley: University of California Press, 1999).

11. See figure-competition1.blogspot.ca/2009/10/brief-history-of-figure-bodybuilding.html (accessed 7 January 2011).

12. Although figure girls have yet to be studied ethnographically or quantitatively, a recent publication by Anne Bolin argues that figure competitions are meant to counteract the more unsettling physiques of heavyweight female bodybuilders. Her "Buff Bodies and the Beast: Emphasized Femininity, Labor, and Power Relations among Fitness, Figure, and Women Bodybuilding Competitors 1985–2010" in *Critical Readings in Bodybuilding,* eds. Adam Locks and Niall Richardson (New York: Routledge, 2012), 29–57, also offers a brief history of figure contests. For other short discussions of the invention and promotion of figure girls see Tanya Bunsell, *Strong and Hard Women: An Ethnography of Female Bodybuilding* (London: Routledge, 2013), 34–38, and Dewaldt Koekemoer, "A Brief History of Figure Bodybuilding," *Ezine Articles* (1 October 2009): http://ezinearticles.com/?A-Brief-History-of-Figure-Bodybuilding&id=3017779 (accessed 26 October 2013).

13. See, for example, Eugene Y. Wang, "Watching the Steps: Peripatetic Vision in Medieval China," in *Visuality Before and Beyond the Renaissance: Seeing as Others Saw,* ed. Robert S. Nelson, (Cambridge: Cambridge University Press, 1997), 116–42, Jonathan Crary, *Techniques of the Observer: On Vision and Modernity in the Nineteenth Century* (Cambridge, MA: MIT Press, 1990), and Lianne McTavish, "Learning to See in New Brunswick, 1862–1929," *Canadian Historical Review* 87, 4 (December 2006): 553–81.

14. Hal Foster, "Preface," *Vision and Visuality,* ed. Hal Foster (Seattle, WA: Bay Press, 1988), ix.

15. Sarah Franklin, "Rethinking Nature/Culture: Anthropology and the New Genetics," *Anthropological Theory* 3, 1 (2003): 65–85.

16. Cressida Heyes, "Foucault Goes to Weight Watchers," *Hypatia* 21, 2 (2006): 126–49.

17. Sarah Strauss, *Positioning Yoga: Balancing Acts Across Cultures* (Oxford: Berg, 2005).

18. Lola Williamson, *Transcendent in America: Hindu-Inspired Meditation Movements as New* Religion (New York: New York University Press, 2010).

19. Frédéric Delvaier, *Women's Strength Training Anatomy* (Champaign, IL: Human Kinetics, 2003).

20. Sessions, *Figure Competition Secrets* (http://www.figurecompetitionsecrets.com/?hop=index40).

21. Sessions, *Figure Competition Secrets* (http://www.figurecompetitionsecrets.com/?hop=index40).

22. See Lianne McTavish, *Childbirth and the Display of Authority in Early Modern France* (Aldershot: Ashgate, 2005).

23. In 1726 Mary Toft (also spelled Tofts) temporarily fooled doctors into believing she had given birth to a litter of rabbits. See Dennis Todd, *Imagining Monsters: Miscreations of the Self in Eighteenth-Century England* (Chicago, IL: University of Chicago Press, 1995).

24. yoga.lovetoknow.com/Interview_with_Yoga_Expert_Kate_Potter (accessed 6 January 2011).

25. Strauss, *Positioning Yoga,* 54, discusses the "oasis regime" of this kind of retreat yoga training.

26. Pierre Bourdieu, *Distinction: A Social Critique of the Judgment of Taste,* trans. Richard Nice (Cambridge, MA: Harvard University Press, 1984).

27. Cressida J. Heyes, *Self-Transformations: Foucault, Ethics, and Normalized Bodies* (Oxford: Oxford University Press, 2007), 129.

28. www.weightwatchers.ca/plan/apr/index.aspx (accessed 6 January 2011).

29. www.weightwatchers.ca/plan/apr/index.aspx (accessed 6 January 2011).

30. Heyes, "Foucault Goes to Weight Watchers."

31. See Leslie Heywood, *Bodymakers: A Cultural Anatomy of Women's Body Building* (New Brunswick, NJ: Rutgers University Press, 1998).

32. For example, see http://www.artofliving.org/yoga/yoga-and-food/yoga-food; http://www.yogicameron.com/what-is-ayurveda; http://www.lemondrop.com/2010/08/11/i-tried-the-ayurveda-diet-road-test.

33. For a discussion of the medical nature of the early modern diet, see Lianne McTavish, "Reproduction and Regulation in Early

Modern Europe," in *The Routledge History of Sex and the Body in the West, 1500 to the Present,* eds. Sarah Toulalan and Kate Fisher (New York: Routledge, 2013), 351–71.

34. www.weightwatchers.ca/util/art/index_art.aspx?tabnum=1& art_id=19821 (accessed 7 January 2011).

35. Heidi Rimke, "Governing Citizens through Self-Help Literature," *Cultural Studies* 14, 1 (2000): 61–78.

36. Heyes, "Foucault Goes to Weight Watchers."

Chapter Two. Embodiment and the Event of Muscle Failure

1. Maurice Merleau-Ponty, *Nature: Course Notes from the Collège de France,* ed. Dominique Ségland, trans. Robert Vallier (Evanston, IL: Northwestern University Press, 2003), 69.

2. For Cassils's curriculum vitae see cassils.wordpress.com/cv/ (accessed 25 July 2012).

3. I thank Nicole Glenn for pointing out that Cassils also implies that categories, such as those related to gender and sexuality, must also be broken down in order for transformation to occur. I consider this possibility in Chapter Four.

4. For a more detailed definition of muscle failure see www. livestrong.com/article/405318-types-of-muscle-failure-in-bodybuilding/ (accessed 25 July 2012).

5. I thank Anne Whitelaw for drawing my attention to the humanizing effect of Cassils's expressions in this video.

6. Eileen Kennedy and Pirkko Markula, eds., *Women and Exercise: The Body, Health and Consumerism* (New York: Routledge, 2011), 1–25.

7. See, for example, Leslie Heywood, "Producing Girls: Empire, Sport, and the Neoliberal Body," in *Physical Culture, Power, and the Body,* eds. Jennifer Hargreaves and Patricia Vertinsky (New York: Routledge, 2007), 101–19, and Susan Bordo, *Unbearable Weight: Feminism, Western Culture, and the Body* (Berkeley, CA: University of California Press, 2003), 14–15.

8. Pirkko Markula, "Postmodern Aerobics," in *Athletic Intruders: Ethnographic Research on Women, Culture, and Exercise,* eds. Anne Bolin and Jane Granskog (Albany, NY: The State University of New York Press, 2003), 54–77.

9. Samantha Holland, *Pole Dancing, Empowerment, and Embodiment* (New York: Palgrave Macmillan, 2010).

10. Barbara Duden, *The Woman Beneath the Skin: A Doctor's Patients in Eighteenth-Century Germany* (Cambridge, MA: Harvard University Press, 1991).

11. For an overview of the shifting historical conceptions of the body see Emily Martin, *Flexible Bodies: Tracking Immunity in American Culture from the Days of Polio to the Age of AIDS* (Boston, MA: Beacon Press, 1994).

12. Dorothea Olkowski and Gail Weiss, eds., *Feminist Interpretations of Maurice Merleau-Ponty* (University Park, PA: The Pennsylvania State University Press, 2006), Johanna Oksala, "A Phenomenology of Gender," *Continental Philosophy Review* 39, 3 (2006): 229–44, and Judith Butler, "Performative Acts and Gender Constitution: An Essay in Phenomenology and Feminist Theory," in *The Feminist Philosophy Reader,* eds. Alison Bailey and Chris Cuomo (Boston, MA: McGraw-Hill, 2008), 97–107.

13. Sebastian Luft and Soren Overgaard, "Introduction," in *The Routledge Companion to Phenomenology,* eds. Sebastian Luft and Soren Overgaard (New York: Routledge, 2012), 1–15.

14. For an overview of Husserl's work see Burt C. Hopkins, *The Philosophy of Husserl* (Durham: Acumen, 2011).

15. Sara Heinämaa, *Toward a Phenomenology of Sexual Difference: Husserl, Merleau-Ponty, Beauvoir* (Lanham, MD: Rowman and Littlefield Publishers, 2003).

16. Komarine Romdenh-Romluc, "Maurice Merleau-Ponty," in *The Routledge Companion to Phenomenology,* eds. Luft and Overgaard, 107.

17. Komarine Romdenh-Romluc, "Maurice Merleau-Ponty," 103–12.

18. Heinämaa, *Toward a Phenomenology of Sexual Difference.*

19. Heinämaa, *Toward a Phenomenology of Sexual Difference.*, xi.

20. Judith Butler, "Sex and Gender in Simone de Beauvoir's *Second Sex,*" *Yale French Studies* (Winter 1986): 35–49.

21. Butler, "Sex and Gender in Simone de Beauvoir's *Second Sex.*"

22. Simone de Beauvoir, *The Second Sex,* trans. H. M. Parshley (London: Four Square Books, 1960).

23. Iris Marion Young, "Throwing Like a Girl: A Phenomenology of Feminine Body Comportment, Motility, and Spatiality," in *Throwing Like a Girl and Other Essays in Feminist Philosophy and Social Theory* (Bloomington, IN: Indiana University Press, 1990), 146–47. There have been many feminist responses to and critiques of the arguments made by Iris Marion Young, including Ann Ferguson and Mechthild Nagel, eds., *Dancing with Iris: The Philosophy of Iris Marion Young* (Oxford: Oxford University Press, 2009), Silvia Stoller, "Reflections on Feminist Merleau-Ponty Skepticism," *Hypatia* 15, 1 (Winter 2000): 175–82, and Tanya Bunsell, *Strong and Hard Women: An Ethnography of Female Bodybuilding* (London: Routledge, 2013), 10–12.

24. Dianne Chisholm, "Climbing Like a Girl: An Exemplary Adventure in Feminist Phenomenology," *Hypatia* 23, 1 (2008): 9–40.

25. Edmund Husserl, "Perception, Spatiality, and the Body," in *The Essential Husserl: Basic Writings in Transcendental Phenomenology*, ed. Donn Welton (Bloomington, IN: Indiana University Press, 1999), 184.

26. *The Essential Husserl*, 179.

27. *The Essential Husserl*, 178.

28. *The Essential Husserl*, 176.

29. See the first chapter of Martin Jay, *Downcast Eyes: The Denigration of Vision in Twentieth-Century French Thought* (Berkeley, CA: University of California Press, 1993).

30. I thank Nicole Glenn for informing me that phenomenological theories, including those based on the work of Heidegger, include multiple physical sensations as well as those forgotten or ignored among their purview.

31. Taylor Carman, "The Body in Husserl and Merleau-Ponty," *Philosophical Topics* 27, 2 (1999): 205–26.

32. "The Body in Husserl and Merleau-Ponty," 219.

33. "The Body in Husserl and Merleau-Ponty," 220.

34. "The Body in Husserl and Merleau-Ponty," 220.

35. Michel Foucault, *History of Madness*, trans. Jonathan Murphy and Jean Khalfa (New York: Routledge, 2006).

36. David M. Halperin, *Saint Foucault: Towards a Gay Hagiography* (New York: Oxford University Press, 1995).

37. For a definition of endorphins see The Free Online Dictionary: medical-dictionary.thefreedictionary.com/Endorphin+rush (accessed 25 July 2012).

38. For the study by Debby Herbenick at Indiana University see medicalxpress.com/news/2012-03-female-orgasm-sexual-pleasure.html (accessed 25 July 2012).

39. Michel Foucault, *The History of Sexuality: An Introduction,* vol. 1, trans. Robert Hurley (New York: Vintage Books, 1990), 157.

40. Anonymous comment made in response to the post "The Sexualization of Female Athletes," 16 June 2012 on feministfigure-girl.com (accessed 25 July 2012).

41. See, for example, Adele E. Clarke, et al., eds., *Biomedicalization: Technoscience, Health, and Illness in the U. S.* (Durham, NC: Duke University Press, 2010).

42. Anonymous comment made in response to the post "The Sexualization of Female Athletes," 16 June 2012 on feministfigure-girl.com (accessed 25 July 2012).

43. See www.haescommunity.org (accessed 25 July 2012).

Chapter Three. Replacing Feminism

1. For a definition of an indexical visual sign see Charles Sanders Peirce, "Sign," in *Peirce on Signs: Writings on Semiotics by Charles Sanders Peirce,* ed. James Hoopes (Chapel Hill, NC: University of North Carolina Press, 1991), 239–40.

2. See, for example, Marcia Ian, "From Abject to Object: Women's Bodybuilding," *Postmodern Culture* 1, 3 (May 1991): 1–10, Dayna B. Daniels, "Gender (Body) Verification (Building)," *Play and Culture* 5 (1992): 370–77, Sharon R. Guthrie and Shirley Castelnuovo, "Elite Women Bodybuilders: Models of Resistance or Compliance?" *Play and Culture* 5 (1992): 401–408, Alan Mansfield and Barbara McGinn, "Pumping Irony: The Muscular and the Feminine," in *Body Matters: Essays on the Sociology of the Body,* eds. Sue Scott and David Morgan (London: Falmer Press, 1993), 49–68, Leena St. Martin and Nicola Gavey, "Women's Bodybuilding: Feminist Resistance and/or Femininity's Recuperation?" *Body and Society* 2, 4 (1996): 45–57, M. Ann Hall, *Feminism and Sporting Bodies* (Champaign, IL: Human

Kinetics, 1996), 59–63, Anne Bolin, "Flex Appeal, Food, and Fat: Competitive Bodybuilding, Gender, and Diet," in *Building Bodies*, ed. Pamela L. Moore (Rutgers, NB: Rutgers University Press, 1997), 184–208, Leslie Heywood, *Bodymakers: A Cultural Anatomy of Women's Body Building* (New Brunswick, NJ: Rutgers University Press, 1998), Maria R. Lowe, *Women of Steel: Female Bodybuilders and the Struggle for Self-Definition* (New York: New York University Press, 1998), Jenny Ryan, "Muscling In: Gender and Physicality in Weight-training Culture," in *Reframing the Body*, ed. Nick Watson (New York: Palgrave, 2001), 166–86, Cindy Patton, "'Rock Hard': Judging the Female Physique," *Journal of Sport and Social Issues* 25, 2 (May 2001): 118–40, Jacqueline Brady, "Is a Hard Woman Good to Find? Reconsidering the Modern Amazon Project," *Studies in Gender and Sexuality* 2, 3 (2001): 215–41, Marcia Ian, "The Primitive Subject of Female Bodybuilding: Transgression and Other Postmodern Myths," *Differences: A Journal of Feminist Cultural Studies* 12, 3 (2001): 69–100, Camilla Obel, "Collapsing Gender in Competitive Bodybuilding: Researching Contradictions and Ambiguity in Sport," in *Gender and Sport: A Reader*, eds. Shelia Scraton and Anne Flintoff (London: Routledge, 2002), 241–54, Anne Bolin, "Beauty or the Beast: The Subversive Soma," in *Athletic Intruders: Ethnographic Research on Women, Culture, and Exercise*, eds. Anne Bolin and Jane Granskog (Albany, NY: State University of New York Press, 2003), 107–29, Jan Brace-Govan, "Weighty Matters: Control of Women's Access to Physical Strength," *The Sociological Review* (2004): 503–31, Gordon B. Forbes, et al., "Perceptions of the Social and Personal Characteristics of Hypermuscular Women and of the Men Who Love Them," *The Journal of Social Psychology* 144, 5 (2004): 487–506, Marla Morton-Brown, "Artificial Ef-femination: Female Bodybuilding and Gender Disruption," *Philosophy in the Contemporary World* 11, 1 (2004): 25–33, Lex Boyle, "Flexing the Tensions of Female Muscularity: How Female Bodybuilders Negotiate Normative Femininity in Competitive Bodybuilding," *Women's Studies Quarterly* 33, 1/2 (Spring-Summer 2005): 134–49, and Shelly A. McGrath and Ruth A. Chananie-Hill, "'Big Freaky-Looking Women': Normalizing Gender Transgression Through Bodybuilding," *Sociology of Sport Journal* 26 (2009): 235–54.

3. Peggy Roussel, Jean Griffet, and Pascal Duret, "The Decline of Female Bodybuilding in France," *Sociology of Sport Journal* 20 (2003): 40–59, Niall Richardson, "The Queer Activity of Extreme Male Bodybuilding: Gender Dissidence, Auto-eroticism and Hysteria," *Social Semiotics* 14, 1 (April 2004): 49–63, Claudia Schippert, "Can Muscles be Queer? Reconsidering the Transgressive Hyper-built Body," *Journal of Gender Studies* 16, 2 (July 2007): 155–71, and Niall Richardson, *Transgressive Bodies: Representations in Film and Popular Culture* (Burlington, VT: Ashgate, 2010), 25–72.

4. Heidi J. Nast and Steve Pile, "Introduction," in *Places Through the Body*, eds. Heidi J. Nast and Steve Pile (London: Routledge, 1998), 1.

5. See, for example, Pauli Tapani Karjalainen and Pauline von Bonsdorff, *Place and Embodiment* (Helsinki: University of Helsinki, 1995), and Tim Cresswell, *Place: A Short Introduction* (Maldon, MA: Blackwell, 2004).

6. I address theories of performance and examples of performance art in more detail in Chapter Four of this book.

7. The Feminist Figure Girl project was discussed in numerous national and international media publications as well as on radio programs, representations that are considered more fully in Chapters Four and Five of this book. See, for example, Sarah Boesveld, "Muscular Feminism," *National Post* (28 June 2011): A3.

8. For a good overview of the multiple meanings attached to the term postfeminism see Stéphanie Genz and Benjamin A. Brabon, "Introduction," *Postfeminism: Cultural Texts and Theories* (Edinburgh: Edinburgh University Press, 2009), 1–50.

9. Patricia Mann, *Micro-politics: Agency in a Post-Feminist Era* (Minneapolis, MN: University of Minnesota Press, 1994), 114.

10. Jessie Givner, "Reproducing Reproductive Discourse: Optical Technologies in The Silent Scream and Eclipse of Reason," *Journal of Popular Culture* 28 (Winter 1994): 229–44, Robyn Longhurst, "(Re)presenting Shopping Centres and Bodies: Questions of Pregnancy," in *New Frontiers of Space, Bodies and Gender*, ed. Rosa Ainley (London: Routledge, 1998), 20–34, Elaine Gale Gerber, "RU 486: French Women's Experience of Abortion and Embodiment" (PhD dissertation, University of California, Los

Angeles, 1999), Mark Jackson, *Infanticide: Historical Perspectives on Child Murder and Concealment, 1550–2000* (Aldershot: Ashgate, 2002), Winny Koster, *Secret Strategies: Women and Abortion in Yoruba Society, Nigeria* (Amsterdam: Aksant, 2003), Nie Jing-Bao, *Behind the Silence: Chinese Voices on Abortion* (Lanham: Rowman and Littlefield, 2005), Lianne McTavish, *Childbirth and the Display of Authority in Early Modern France* (Aldershot: Ashgate, 2005), and Robyn Longhurst, *Maternities: Gender, Bodies and Space* (New York: Routledge, 2008).

11. Judy Rebick, *Ten Thousand Roses: The Making of a Feminist Revolution* (Toronto: Penguin, 2005), and Childbirth by Choice Trust, *No Choice: Women Tell Their Stories of Illegal Abortion* (Toronto: Childbirth by Choice Trust, 1998).

12. For more information about this extreme American antiabortion group and its leader, Randall Terry, see Susan Faludi, *Backlash: The Undeclared War Against American Women* (New York: Three Rivers Press, 2006), 409–33.

13. Abortion Rights Coalition of Canada, "Clinic Funding—Overview of Political Situation," Position Paper 3, 2005. http://www.arcc-cdac.ca (accessed 8 November 2013), Abortion Rights Coalition of Canada, "New Brunswick Abortion Access," 2007. http://www.arcc-cdac.ca/news_canadianabortion.html (accessed 8 November 2013), and Anon., "Abortion Panel Issue," *The Daily Gleaner* (26 April 2002).

14. Government of Canada, Health Care System, Canada Health Act, 2005. http://www.hc-sc.gc.ca/hcs-sss/medi-assur/cha-lcs/index-eng.php (accessed 8 November 2013).

15. For a discussion of abortion policy in Canada see Lianne McTavish, "The Cultural Production of Pregnancy: Bodies and Embodiment at a New Brunswick Abortion Clinic," *Topia: Canadian Journal of Cultural Studies* 20 (Fall 2008): 23–42, and Howard A. Palley, "Canadian Abortion Policy: National Policy and the Impact of Federalism and Political Implementation on Access to Services," *Publius: The Journal of Federalism* 36, 4 (2006): 565–86.

16. Shannon Hagerman, "Abortion Lawsuit On," *The Daily Gleaner* (24 October 2002), Shannon Hagerman, "Policy Unchanged. Blaney Doesn't Believe Abortion Access Limited," *The Daily Gleaner* (8 November 2002), Stephen Llewellyn, "N. B. Says

Funded Abortions Available; Concern—Some People Believe Access to Abortion is Too Limited in Province," *The Daily Gleaner* (19 May 2006).

17. Personal communication with Judy Burwell, director of the Morgentaler Clinic in Fredericton (1999–2005), 2007. She now volunteers at the clinic. See also Laura Eggerston, "Abortion Services in Canada: A Patchwork Quilt with Many Holes," *Canadian Medical Association Journal* (20 March 2001): 847–49. http://www.cmaj.ca/content/64/6/847.full (accessed 8 November 2013), and Joanna N. Erdman, "In the Back Alleys of Health Care: Abortion, Equality, and Community in Canada," *Emory Law Journal* 56, 4 (2007): 1093–1156.

18. Abortion Rights Coalition of Canada, "How do Crisis Pregnancy Centres Mislead Women?" pamphlet, 2005. http://www. arcc-cdac.ca/action/CPC-borchure.pdf (accessed 8 November 2013).

19. Jody Berland, "Weathering the North: Climate, Colonialism, and the Mediated Body," in *Relocating Cultural Studies: Developments in Theory and Research*, eds. Valda Blundell, John Shepherd, and Ian Taylor (London: Routledge, 1993), 207–25.

20. Carroll Smith-Rosenberg, "Constituting Nations/Violently Excluding Women: The First Contract with America," in *Virtual Gender: Fantasies of Subjectivity and Embodiment*, eds. Mary Ann O'Farrell and Lynne Vallone (Ann Arbor, MI: University of Michigan Press, 1999), 171–89.

21. Katherine N. Hayles, *How We Became Posthuman: Virtual Bodies in Cybernetics, Literature, and Informatics* (Chicago, IL: Chicago University Press, 1999), 196.

22. Joyce Arthur, "Abortion in Canada: History, Law, and Access," 1999. http://www.prochoiceactionnetwork-canada.org/articles/canada.shtml (accessed 8 November 2013).

23. McTavish, "The Cultural Production of Pregnancy."

24. Personal communication with Gillian Kovack, 2008.

25. See www.abba.ab.ca. Accessed 24 September 2012.

26. Many articles have been written about this film. See, for example, Douglas Sadao Aoki, "Posing the Subject: Sex, Illumination, and *Pumping Iron II: The Women*," *Cinema Journal* 38, 4 (Summer 1999): 24–44.

27. Lesley Fishwick, "Be What You Wanna Be: A Sense of Identity

Down at the Local Gym," in *Reframing the Body*, ed. Nick Watson, 152–65.

28. See www.downsizefitness.com (accessed 8 November 2013).

29. Margaret Shalma, "Resistance Training: Re-Reading Fat Embodiment at a Women's Gym," *Disability Studies Quarterly* 28, 4 (Fall 2008): 1–10.

30. See, for example, Jana Evans Braziel and Kathleen LeBesco, eds., *Bodies out of Bounds: Fatness and Transgression* (Berkeley, CA: University of California Press, 2001), and Esther Rothblum and Sandra Solovay, eds., *The Fat Studies Reader* (New York: New York University Press, 2009).

31. Pirkko Markula, "Firm but Shapely, Fit but Sexy, Strong but Thin: The Postmodern Aerobicizing Female Bodies," *Sociology of Sport Journal*, 12 (1995): 424–53, and Lesley Haravon Collins, "Working Out the Contradiction: Feminism and Aerobics," *Journal of Sport and Social Issues* 26 (February 2002): 85–109.

32. Darrin Clement, "Muscle Memory: Can Muscles Actually Remember?" ezinearticles.com/?Muscle-Memory---Can-Muscles-Actually-Remember?&id=1972308 (accessed 8 November 2013).

33. Pierre Bourdieu, *The Field of Cultural Production: Essays on Art and Literature* (New York: Columbia University Press, 1993).

34. Almost every study of female bodybuilding focuses on the appearance of female practitioners, especially in terms of posing. See note 2 for this chapter above.

35. At one scholarly presentation, a feminist professor asked me why my bodybuilding project had been covered in local and national newspaper reports, featuring me wearing a bikini, whereas her research study had not received any media attention.

36. Lianne McTavish, "Complicating Categories: Women, Gender and Sexuality in Seventeenth-Century French Visual Culture" (PhD dissertation, University of Rochester, 1996).

37. Dewaldt Koekemoer, "A Brief History of Figure Bodybuilding," *Ezine Articles* (1 October 2009): http://ezinearticles.com/?A-Brief-History-of-Figure-Bodybuilding&id=3017779 (accessed 26 October 2013).

38. Lianne McTavish, "It Happened in Las Vegas #2: Bashing the Bikini," *Feminist Figure Girl's Blog* (29 September 2010). femnistfiguregirl.com (accessed 24 September 2012).

39. Judith Butler, *Gender Trouble: Feminism and the Subversion of Identity* (New York: Routledge, 1996).

40. Judith Butler, "Performative Acts and Gender Constitution: An Essay in Phenomenology and Feminist Theory," *Theatre Journal* 40, 4 (December 1988): 520.

41. Butler, "Performative Acts and Gender Constitution," 526.

42. See, for example, Kathleen Rowe Karlyn, "Feminism in the Classroom: Teaching Towards the Third Wave," in *Feminism in Popular Culture*, eds. Joanne Hollows and Rachel Moseley (Oxford: Berg, 2006), 57–75.

43. Joanne Hollows and Rachel Moseley, "Popularity Contests: The Meanings of Popular Feminism," in *Feminism in Popular Culture*, eds. Joanne Hollows and Rachel Moseley), 13, and Shelley Budgeon, "Introduction: Defining the Third Wave," *Third Wave Feminism and the Politics of Gender in Late Modernity* (New York: Palgrave Macmillan, 2011), 1–21. See also Stacy Gillis, Gillian Howie, and Rebecca Munford, *Third Wave Feminism: A Critical Exploration* (New York: Palgrave Macmillan, 2007). In a post in August 2010 on my blog site, feministfiguregirl.com, called "Oh Shit, Am I a Third Wave Feminist?" I pondered what I felt was a decidedly unpleasant possibility, affirming that the answer was mostly no.

44. Jonathan Dean, *Rethinking Contemporary Feminist Politics* (New York: Palgrave Macmillan, 2010).

45. Angela McRobbie, *The Aftermath of Feminism: Gender, Culture, and Social Change* (London: Sage, 2009), 85.

46. David Harvey, *A Brief History of Neoliberalism* (Oxford: Oxford University Press, 2005).

47. For a discussion of fitspiration posters within the context of neoliberalism, see a post published in December 2012 on my blog site, feministfiguregirl.com, called "The 'Fat' Female Body (in Pursuit of Happiness)."

48. Louise Owen, "'Work that Body': Precarity and Femininity in the New Economy," *TDR: The Drama Review* 56, 4 (Winter 2012): 78–94.

49. Samantha Holland, *Pole Dancing, Empowerment, and Embodiment* (New York: Palgrave Macmillan, 2010).

50. For arguments that position cosmetic surgery as a tool of patriarchal oppression see Naomi Wolf, *The Beauty Myth: How Images of*

Beauty are Used Against Women (Toronto: Random House, 1990), and Kathryn Pauly Morgan, "Women and the Knife: Cosmetic Surgery and the Colonization of Women's Bodies," *Hypatia* 6, 3 (Autumn 1991): 25–53. For some ethnographic and sociological accounts of cosmetic procedures see Kathy Davis, *Reshaping the Female Body: The Dilemma of Cosmetic Surgery* (New York: Routledge, 1995), Victoria Pitts-Taylor, *Surgery Junkies: Wellness and Pathology in Cosmetic Culture* (New Brunswick, NJ: Rutgers University Press, 2007), and Rhian Parker, *Women, Doctors and Cosmetic Surgery: Negotiating the 'Normal' Body* (New York: Palgrave Macmillan, 2010). For comparative discussions see Debra Gimlin, *Cosmetic Surgery Narratives: A Cross-Cultural Analysis of Women's Accounts* (New York: Palgrave McMillan, 2012), and Cressida J. Heyes and Meredith Jones, eds., *Cosmetic Surgery: A Feminist Primer* (Aldershot: Ashgate, 2009).

51. Heyes and Jones, eds., *Cosmetic Surgery.* See also my post from November 2010, "The Look of Cosmetic Surgery" at feministfiguregirl,com.

52. Tanya Bunsell, *Strong and Hard Women: An Ethnography of Female Bodybuilding* (London: Routledge, 2013).

53. Genz and Brabon, *Postfeminism: Cultural Texts and Theories.* See also Nancy A. Hewitt, *No Permanent Waves: Recasting Histories of U.S. Feminism* (New Brunswick, NJ: Rutgers University Press, 2010), and Rosalind Gill, *New Femininities: Postfeminism, Neoliberalism, and Subjectivity* (New York: Palgrave MacMillan, 2011).

54. Mann, *Micro-politics*, 208.

55. See, for example, Jane Pilcher, *50 Key Concepts in Gender Studies* (Thousand Oaks, CA: Sage, 2004).

Chapter Four. On Stage

1. Simone de Beauvoir, *The Second Sex*, trans. H. M. Parshley (London: Four Square Books, 1960), 377.

2. *The Second Sex*, 376.

3. *The Second Sex*, 376.

4. Amelia Jones, "The Now and the Has Been: Paradoxes of Live Art in History," in *Perform, Repeat, Record: Live Art in History,*

eds. Amelia Jones and Adrian Heathfield (Bristol: Intellect, 2012), 12.

5. Kristine Stiles, Klaus Biesenbach, and Chrissie Iles, *Marina Abramović* (London: Phaidon, 2008), 12–13, and Mary Richards, *Marina Abramović* (New York: Routledge, 2010), 83–93.

6. Richards, *Marina Abramović*, 22.

7. Marina Abramović, *Marina Abramović: The Artist is Present* (New York: Museum of Modern Art, 2010), and Matthew Akers and Jeff Dupre, *Marina Abramović: The Artist is Present* (New York: Show of Force LLC and Mudpuppy Films, Inc., 2012).

8. Heather Cassils, "About," www.heathercassils.com/#ABOUT (accessed 30 December 2012). See also Julia Steinmetz, Heather Cassils, and Clover Leary, "Behind Enemy Lines: Toxic Titties Infiltrate Vanessa Beecroft," *Signs: Journal of Women in Culture and Society* (Spring 2003): 753–83.

9. Heather Cassils, "Cuts: A Traditional Sculpture," www.heathercassils.com/#cuts-a-traditional-sculpture-2011 (accessed 30 December 2012).

10. Judith Butler, "Performative Acts and Gender Constitution: An Essay in Phenomenology and Feminist Theory," *Theatre Journal* 40, 4 (December 1988): 521: "As an intentionally organized materiality, the body is always an embodying *of* possibilities both conditioned and circumscribed by historical convention."

11. See, for example, Hans Ulrich-Obrist, *Marina Abramović* (Cologne: W. König, 2010), and James Westcott, *When Marina Abramović Dies: A Biography* (Cambridge: MIT Press, 2010).

12. Thomas McEvilley, *Art, Love, Friendship, Marina Abramovic and Ulay: Together and Apart* (New York: McPherson and Company, 2010), 44–46, and Richards, *Marina Abramović*, 93–99.

13. Jason Edward Kaufman, "Abramovic's School for Performance Art," *Art Newspaper* 16 (December 2007): 1.

14. Anna Danieri, et al., *Marina Abramović* (Milan: Charta, 2002), 52.

15. Johan Pijnappel, "Marina Abramovic, Reflections on the Mental Conditioning of the Artist," *Art and Design* 9 (September/October 1994): 48–55.

16. Pijnappel, "Marina Abramovic, Reflections on the Mental Conditioning of the Artist," 48–55.

17. Karen Sessions, *Figure Competition Secrets* (Karen Sessions Inc., 2010).

18. My insistence on the necessity of competing at least once is at odds with other definitions of bodybuilding. See, for example, Niall Richardson, "Introduction to Part 1: What is the 'Practice' of Bodybuilding?" in *Critical Readings in Bodybuilding*, eds. Adam Locks and Niall Richardson (New York: Routledge, 2012), 21–28.

19. I went through all the ethics protocols at the University of Alberta before undertaking any participant observation in this and all other cases cited in this book.

20. Rudolph Bell, *Holy Anorexia* (Chicago: University of Chicago Press, 1987), and Caroline Walker Bynum, *Holy Feast and Holy Fast: The Religious Significance of Food to Medieval Women* (Berkeley: University of California Press, 1987).

21. Michel Foucault, *Discipline and Punish: The Birth of the Prison*, trans. Alan Sheridan (New York: Vintage, 1977), 5–6.

22. See, for example, Gabriella Giannachi, Nick Kaye, and Michael Shanks, eds., *Archaeologies of Presence: Art, Performance and the Persistence of Being* (London: Routledge, 2012).

23. Amelia Jones, "Temporal Anxiety/'Presence' in *Absentia*: Experiencing Performance as Documentation," in *Archaeologies of Presence*, eds. Giannachi, Kaye, and Shanks, 197–221.

24. For an account of the increasingly widespread demand for the performance of emotional labor in corporatized venues see George Ritzer, *The McDonaldization of Society* (Thousand Oaks, CA: Sage, 2013).

25. Heather Cassils, "Cuts: A Traditional Sculpture," www.heather-cassils.com/#cuts-a-traditional-sculpture-2011 (accessed 31 December 2012).

26. Heather Cassils, "The Body as Social Sculpture," unpublished artist's talk given at the University of Alberta, 8 November 2012.

27. Peggy Phelan, ed., *Live Art in LA: Performance in Southern California, 1970–1983* (New York: Routledge, 2012), 184, fn. 119, describes Cassils's *Cuts* as a commission for a show at LACE (Los Angeles Contemporary Exhibitions) called "Los Angeles Goes Live: Performance Art in Southern California, 1970–1983," from 27 September 2011–29 January 2012, noting that it drew on the work of Eleanor Antin as well as Lynda Benglis. See

also Cherise Smith, *Enacting Others: Politics of Identity in Eleanor Antin, Nikki S. Lee, Adrian Piper, and Anna Deavere Smith* (Durham, NC: Duke University Press, 2011).

28. James Hall, *Michelangelo and the Invention of the Human Body* (New York: Farrar, Straus and Giroux, 2005).

29. Robin Black and Heather Cassils, "Lady Face//Man Body" www.ladyfacemanbody.com (accessed 31 December 2012).

30. Susan N. Richmond, "Sizing up the Dildo: Lynda Benglis' 1974 *Artforum* Advertisement as a Feminist Icon," *Paradoxa* 15 (2005): 24–34.

31. Sigmund Freud, "Fetishism (1927)," *Sexuality and the Psychology of Love* (New York: Macmillan, 1963), 214–19.

32. For the anonymous comments on Cassils's *Cuts* see www.youtube.com/watch?v=RZFumYzWYGA (accessed 31 December 2012).

33. Joanna Woods-Marsden, *Renaissance Self-Portraiture: The Visual Construction of Identity and Social Status of the Artist* (New Haven, CT: Yale University Press, 1998).

34. Anne Hollander, *Seeing Through Clothes* (Berkeley: University of California Press, 1993), and Marcia Ian, "How Do You Wear Your Body? Bodybuilding and the Sublimity of Drag," in *Negotiating Lesbian and Gay Subjects*, eds. Monica Dorenkamp and Richard Henke (New York: Routledge, 1995), 71–92.

35. Ian, "How Do You Wear Your Body?" 79.

36. Ian, "How Do You Wear Your Body?" 78.

37. See, for example, Susan Stryker and Stephen Whittle, eds., *The Transgender Studies Reader* (New York: Routledge, 2006), and Anne Enke, *Transfeminist Perspectives in and Beyond Transgender and Gender Studies* (Philadelphia, PA: Temple University Press, 2012).

38. See, for example, Marcia Ian, "From Abject to Object: Women's Bodybuilding," *Postmodern Culture* 1, 3 (May 1991): 1–10, Dayna B. Daniels, "Gender (Body) Verification (Building)," *Play and Culture* 5 (1992): 370–77, Sharon R. Guthrie and Shirley Castelnuovo, "Elite Women Bodybuilders: Models of Resistance or Compliance?" *Play and Culture* 5 (1992): 401–8, Leena St. Martin and Nicola Gavey, "Women's Bodybuilding: Feminist Resistance and/or Femininity's Recuperation?" *Body and Society* 2 (1996): 45–57, Jenny Ryan, "Muscling In: Gender

and Physicality in Weight-training Culture," in *Reframing the Body*, ed. Nick Watson (New York: Palgrave, 2001), 166–86, and Camilla Obel, "Collapsing Gender in Competitive Bodybuilding: Researching Contradictions and Ambiguity in Sport," in *Gender and Sport: A Reader*, eds. Shelia Scraton and Anne Flintoff (London: Routledge, 2002), 241–54.

39. Niall Richardson, "The Queer Activity of Extreme Male Bodybuilding: Gender Dissidence, Auto-eroticism and Hysteria," *Social Semiotics* 14, 1 (April 2004): 49–63, and Claudia Schippert, "Can Muscles be Queer? Reconsidering the Transgressive Hyper-built Body," *Journal of Gender Studies* 16, 2 (July 2007): 155–71.

40. John N. Hoberman, *Testosterone Dreams: Rejuvenation, Aphrodisia, Doping* (Berkeley, CA: University of California Press, 2005).

41. Most of the negative comments were posted in response to the online publication of an article about my project in the *National Post* on Tuesday 28 June 2011. They have since been removed from the website, but I kept printed copies of every comment.

42. The most rabid comments were posted on a "men's rights" website called MGTO Forums (Men Going Their Own Way), under the section "Men's General Discussion" on 29 June 2011, in response to the *National Post* article, www.mgtoformums.com (accessed 30 June 2011).

43. Anne Bolin, "Buff Bodies and the Beast: Emphasized Femininity, Labor, and Power Relations among Fitness, Figure, and Women Bodybuilding Competitors 1985–2010," in *Critical Readings in Bodybuilding*, eds. Locks and Richardson, 29–57.

44. Pamela L. Moore, "Feminist Bodybuilding, Sex, and the Interruption of Investigative Knowledge," in *Building Bodies*, ed. Pamela L. Moore (New Brunswick, NJ: Rutgers University Press, 1997), 74–86.

45. Heather Cassils, "Hard Times," www.heathercassils.com/# HARD-TIMES-2010 (accessed 31 December 2012).

46. Heather Cassils, "Hard Times."

47. Heather Cassils, "The Body as Social Sculpture," unpublished artist's talk given at the University of Alberta, 8 November 2012.

48. Lauren Berlant, *Cruel Optimism* (Durham, NC: Duke University Press, 2011), 1.

49. Lauren Berlant, "Slow Death: Obesity, Sovereignty, Lateral Agency," *Cruel Optimism*, 95–119.

50. Judith Butler, *Gender Trouble: Feminism and the Subversion of Identity* (New York: Routledge, 1990).

51. Judith Butler, *Bodies that Matter: On the Discursive Limits of "Sex"* (New York: Routledge, 1993), 32.

Chapter Five. Aftermath

1. For some of the diversity of bodybuilding literature see Chapter Three of this book, notes two and three. Important recent work has considered the often erotic portrayal of female bodybuilders in print and as they "web cam" for fee-paying viewers. See Niall Richardson, "Flex-rated! Female Bodybuilding: Feminist Resistance or Erotic Spectacle?" *Journal of Gender Studies* 17, 4 (December 2008): 289–301, reprinted in his *Transgressive Bodies: Representations in Film and Popular Culture* (Burlington, VT: Ashgate, 2010), 59–72.

2. See, for example, David Green and Joanna Lowry, eds., *Stillness and Time: Photography and the Moving Image* (Brighton: Photoforum and Photoworks, 2006).

3. For a review of some of this work see, Laura Levin, "The Performative Force of Photography," *Photography and Culture* 2, 3 (November 2009): 327–36.

4. John Tagg, *The Disciplinary Frame: Photographic Truths and the Capture of Meaning* (Minneapolis: University of Minnesota Press, 2009).

5. Gillian Rose, *Visual Methodologies* (London: Sage, 2001), 16–28.

6. For a definition of an iconic visual sign see Charles Sanders Peirce, "Sign," in *Peirce on Signs: Writings on Semiotics by Charles Sanders Peirce*, ed. James Hoopes (Chapel Hill, NC: University of North Carolina Press, 1991), 251–52.

7. Charles Sanders Peirce, "Sign," 239–40.

8. See, for instance, Corey Dzenko, "The Indexical Function of Photographic Images," *Afterimage* 37, 2 (September/October 2009): 19–23.

9. Susan Sontag, *On Photography* (New York: Farrar, Strauss, and Giroux, 1978), 9.

10. Levin, "The Performative Force of Photography," 327–36.

11. J. L. Austin, *How to Do Things with Words* (Oxford: Clarendon, 1962).

12. Levin, "The Performative Force of Photography," 329.

13. John Tagg, *The Burden of Representation: Essays on Photographies and Histories* (Amherst, MA: University of Massachusetts Press, 1988).

14. Diana Fuss, *Identification Papers* (New York: Routledge, 1995), and Judith Halberstam, *Female Masculinity* (Durham: Duke University Press, 1988).

15. For instance, this was one of the reactions to my keynote talk, "Female Embodiment and the Experience of Muscle Failure," given at the Western Humanities Alliance Annual Meeting at the University of California, Merced, 25 October 2012.

16. I received this reaction, among others, to my talk, "Becoming Feminist Figure Girl: Bodybuilding as Research," given as part of the Feminist Research Speakers Series, University of Alberta, Edmonton, AB, 20 October 2011.

17. I received this response to one of my staged photos while Heather Cassils was at the University of Alberta in November 2012 to give a talk called "The Body as Social Sculpture."

18. Along with the other most antifeminist and sexist comments to my project, this image was posted on the website called MGTO Forums (Men Going Their Own Way), under the section "Men's General Discussion" on 29 June 2011 www.mgtoformums.com (accessed 24 June 2011). The forum at www.mgtoformums.com was shut down by its facilitator in February 2014. See http://www.reddit.com/r/TheRedPill/comments/1xkwq6/mgtowforums_shut_down.

19. George Butler, dir., *Pumping Iron II: The Women* (Barbelle, 1985).

20. Rosalind E. Krauss, "Informe without Conclusion," *October* 78 (Fall 1996): 89–105, and Hal Foster, "Obscene, Abject, Traumatic," *October* 78 (Fall 1996): 106–24.

21. Julia Kristeva, *Powers of Horror: An Essay on Abjection*, trans. Leon S. Roudiez (New York: Columbia University Press, 1982), 1–31.

22. Julia Steinmetz, Heather Cassils, and Clover Leary, "Behind Enemy Lines: Toxic Titties Infiltrate Vanessa Beecroft," *Signs: Journal of Women in Culture and Society* (Spring 2003): 753–83.

23. For an introduction to some modern efforts see Amelia Jones, *Body Art: Performing the Subject* (Minneapolis, MN: University of Minnesota Press, 1998).

24. See, for example, Geoffrey Batchen, *Forget Me Not: Photography and Remembrance* (Amsterdam: Van Gogh Museum, 2004), and Catherine Keenan, "On the Relationship between Personal Photographs and Individual Memory," *History of Photography* 22, 1 (Spring 1998): 60–64.

Glossary

bodybuilder—person who lifts weights, trains, and eats methodically in order to obtain an ideally muscular, symmetrical, and proportioned body, primarily for aesthetic purposes often related to his or her participation in bodybuilding competitions. The terms bodybuilder and figure girl are sometimes linked in this book, for the benefit of a general audience, but these categories are clearly differentiated within the culture of physique competitions.

feminist—person with an active political commitment to expanding opportunities and diminishing restrictions in the lives of all women and men, girls and boys.

figure competition—female bodybuilding contest that involves developing a muscular physique with wide shoulders, a small waist, and defined quads but requires a "softer" look than more traditional contests and includes blinged-out bikinis, high heels, and mandatory four-quarter turn poses.

figure girl—a woman who trains for and participates in figure competitions.

glutes—*gluteus maximus*, *gluteus medius*, and *gluteus minimus* muscles, otherwise known as the buttocks, are well developed and round in the body of an ideal figure girl.

hams—the bi-articulate hamstring muscles located at the back of the thigh.

lats—*latissimus dorsi*, the broad, flat muscles on either side of the back, which figure girls deliberately grow through training, and which they flare while competing on stage.

quads—*quadriceps*, the large, four-part extensor muscles at the front of the thigh, which are developed and tensed by figure girls to create a desired "quad sweep" shape in their legs.

Bibliography

Abramović, Marina. *Marina Abramović: The Artist is Present* (New York: Museum of Modern Art, 2010).

Akers, Matthew, and Dupre, Jeff. *Marina Abramović: The Artist is Present* (New York: Show of Force LLC and Mudpuppy Films, Inc., 2012).

Aoki, Douglas Sadao. "Posing the Subject: Sex, Illumination, and *Pumping Iron II: The Women*," *Cinema Journal* 4 (Summer 1999): 24–44.

Austin, J. L. *How to Do Things with Words* (Oxford: Clarendon, 1962).

Balsamo, Anne. "Feminist Bodybuilding," *Technologies of the Gendered Body: Reading Cyborg Women* (Durham, NC: Duke University Press, 1996), 41–55.

Banet-Weiser, Sarah. *The Most Beautiful Girl in the World: Beauty Pageants and National Identity* (Berkeley: University of California Press, 1999).

Batchen, Geoffrey. *Forget Me Not: Photography and Remembrance* (Amsterdam: Van Gogh Museum, 2004).

Beauvoir, Simone de. *The Second Sex*, trans. H. M. Parshley (London: Four Square Books, 1960).

Beauvoir, Simone de, and Young, Iris Marion. *On Female Body Experience: "Throwing Like a Girl" and Other Essays* (New York: Oxford University Press, 2005).

Bell, Rudolph. *Holy Anorexia* (Chicago: University of Chicago Press, 1987).

Berland, Jody. "Weathering the North: Climate, Colonialism, and the Mediated Body," in *Relocating Cultural Studies: Developments in Theory and Research*, eds. Valda Blundell, John Shepherd, and Ian Taylor (London: Routledge, 1993), 207–25.

Berlant, Lauren. *Cruel Optimism* (Durham, NC: Duke University Press, 2011).

Boesveld, Sarah. "Muscular Feminism," *National Post* (28 June 2011): A3.

Bolin, Anne. "Buff Bodies and the Beast: Emphasized Femininity, Labor, and Power Relations among Fitness, Figure, and Women Bodybuilding Competitors 1985–2010," in *Critical Readings in Bodybuilding*, eds. Adam Locks and Niall Richardson (New York: Routledge, 2012), 29–57.

Bolin, Anne. "Flex Appeal, Food, and Fat: Competitive Bodybuilding, Gender, and Diet," in *Building Bodies*, ed. Pamela L. Moore (Rutgers, NB: Rutgers University Press, 1997), 184–208.

Bolin, Anne. "Beauty or the Beast: The Subversive Soma," in *Athletic Intruders: Ethnographic Research on Women, Culture, and Exercise*, eds. Anne Bolin and Jane Granskog (Albany, NY: The State University of New York Press, 2003), 107–29.

Bordo, Susan. *Unbearable Weight: Feminism, Western Culture, and the Body* (Berkeley, CA: University of California Press, 2003).

Bourdieu, Pierre. *Distinction: A Social Critique of the Judgment of Taste* (Cambridge, MA: Harvard University Press, 1984).

Bourdieu, Pierre. *The Field of Cultural Production: Essays on Art and Literature* (New York: Columbia University Press, 1993).

Boyle, Lex. "Flexing the Tensions of Female Muscularity: How Female Bodybuilders Negotiate Normative Femininity in Competitive Bodybuilding," *Women's Studies Quarterly* 33, 1/2 (Spring-Summer 2005): 134–49.

Brady, Jacqueline. "Is a Hard Woman Good to Find? Reconsidering the Modern Amazon Project," *Studies in Gender and Sexuality* 2, 3 (2001): 215–41.

Brace-Govan, Jan. "Weighty Matters: Control of Women's Access to Physical Strength," *The Sociological Review* (2004): 503–31.

Braziel, Jana Evans, and LeBesco, Kathleen, eds. *Bodies out of Bounds: Fatness and Transgression* (Berkeley, CA: University of California Press, 2001).

Brook, Barbara. *Feminist Perspectives on the Body* (London: Longman, 1999).

Budgeon, Shelley. *Third Wave Feminism and the Politics of Gender in Late Modernity* (New York: Palgrave Macmillan, 2011).

Bunsell, Tanya. *Strong and Hard Women: An Ethnography of Female Bodybuilding* (London: Routledge, 2013).

Butler, Judith. "Sex and Gender in Simone de Beauvoir's *Second Sex*," *Yale French Studies* (Winter 1986): 35–49.

Butler, Judith. *Bodies that Matter: On the Discursive Limits of "Sex"* (New York: Routledge, 1993).

Butler, Judith. *Gender Trouble: Feminism and the Subversion of Identity* (New York: Routledge, 1999).

Butler, Judith. "Performative Acts and Gender Constitution: An Essay in Phenomenology and Feminist Theory," *Theatre Journal* 40, 4 (December 1988): 519–31.

Bynum, Caroline Walker. *Holy Feast and Holy Fast: The Religious Significance of Food to Medieval Women* (Berkeley, CA: University of California Press, 1987).

Carman, Taylor. "The Body in Husserl and Merleau-Ponty," *Philosophical Topics* 27, 2 (1999): 205–26.

Chang, Heewon. *Autoethnography as Method* (Walnut Creek, CA: Altamira Press, 2008).

Childbirth by Choice Trust, *No Choice: Women Tell Their Stories of Illegal Abortion* (Toronto: Childbirth by Choice Trust, 1998).

Chisholm, Dianne. "Climbing Like a Girl: An Exemplary Adventure in Feminist Phenomenology," *Hypatia* 23, 1 (2008): 9–40.

Clarke, Adele E., Mamo, Laura, Fosket, Jennifer Ruth, Fishman, Jennifer, and Janet Shim, eds. *Biomedicalization: Technoscience, Health, and Illness in the U. S.* (Durham, NC: Duke University Press, 2010).

Collins, Lesley Haravon. "Working Out the Contradiction: Feminism and Aerobics," *Journal of Sport and Social Issues* 26 (February 2002): 85–109.

Collinson, Jacquelyn Allen, and Hockey, John. "Autoethnography: Self-indulgence or Rigorous Methodology?" *Philosophy and the Sciences of Exercise, Health and Sport: Critical Perspectives on Research Methods* (New York: Routledge, 2005), 187–202.

Crary, Jonathan. *Techniques of the Observer: On Vision and Modernity in the Nineteenth Century* (Cambridge, MA: MIT Press, 1990).

Cresswell, Tim. *Place: A Short Introduction* (Maldon, MA: Blackwell, 2004).

Crossley, Simon. "In the Gym: Motives, Meaning and Moral Careers," *Body and Society* 12 (June 2006): 23–50.

Daniels, Dayna B. "Gender (Body) Verification (Building)," *Play and Culture* 5 (1992): 370–77.

Davis, Kathy. *Reshaping the Female Body: The Dilemma of Cosmetic Surgery* (New York: Routledge, 1995).

Dean, Jonathan, *Rethinking Contemporary Feminist Politics* (New York: Palgrave Macmillan, 2010).

Delvaier, Frédérc. *Women's Strength Training Anatomy* (Champaign, IL: Human Kinetics, 2003).

Duden, Barbara. *The Woman Beneath the Skin: A Doctor's Patients in Eighteenth-Century Germany* (Cambridge, MA: Harvard University Press, 1991).

Dzenko, Corey. "The Indexical Function of Photographic Images," *Afterimage* 37, 2 (September/October 2009): 19–23.

Egan, R. Danielle, Frank, Katherine, and Merri Lisa Johnson, eds. *Flesh for Fantasy: Producing and Consuming Exotic Dance* (New York: Thunder's Mouth Press, 2006).

Ellis, Carolyn. *The Ethnographic I: A Methodological Novel about Autoethnography* (Walnut Creek, CA: Altamira, 2004).

Enke, Anne. *Transfeminist Perspectives in and Beyond Transgender and Gender Studies* (Philadelphia, PA: Temple University Press, 2012).

Faludi, Susan. *Backlash: The Undeclared War Against American Women* (New York: Three Rivers Press, 2006).

Ferguson, Ann, and Nagel, Mechthild, eds. *Dancing with Iris: The Philosophy of Iris Marion Young* (Oxford: Oxford University Press, 2009).

Fishwick, Lesley. "Be What You Wanna Be: A Sense of Identity Down at the Local Gym," in *Reframing the Body*, ed. Nick Watson (New York: Palgrave, 2001), 152–65.

Forbes, Gordon B., et al. "Perceptions of the Social and Personal Characteristics of Hypermuscular Women and of the Men Who Love Them," *The Journal of Social Psychology* 144, 5 (2004): 487–506.

Foster, Hal, ed. *Vision and Visuality* (Seattle, WA: Bay Press, 1988).

Foster, Hal. "Obscene, Abject, Traumatic," *October* 78 (Fall 1996): 106–24.

Foucault, Michel. *Discipline and Punish: The Birth of the Prison*, trans. Alan Sheridan (New York: Vintage, 1979).

Foucault, Michel. *The History of Sexuality: An Introduction*, trans. Robert Hurley (New York: Vintage Books, 1990).

Foucault, Michel. "Governmentality," trans. Rosi Braidotti, in *The Foucault Effect: Studies in Governmentality*, eds. Graham Burchell, Colin Gordon, and Peter Miller (Chicago, IL: University of Chicago Press, 1991), 87–104.

Foucault, Michel. *History of Madness*, trans. Jonathan Murphy and Jean Khalfa (New York: Routledge, 2006).

Franklin, Sarah. "Rethinking Nature/Culture: Anthropology and the New Genetics," *Anthropological Theory* 3, 1 (2003): 65–85.

Freud, Sigmund. "Fetishism (1927)," *Sexuality and the Psychology of Love* (New York: Macmillan, 1963), 214–19.

Fuss, Diana. *Identification Papers* (New York: Routledge, 1995).

Fussell, Samuel Wilson. *Muscle: Confessions of an Unlikely Bodybuilder* (New York: Perennial, 1991).

Genz, Stéphanie, and Brabon, Benjamin A. "Introduction," *Postfeminism: Cultural Texts and Theories* (Edinburgh: Edinburgh University Press, 2009), 1–50.

Gerber, Elaine Gale. "RU 486: French Women's Experience of Abortion and Embodiment" (PhD dissertation, University of California, Los Angeles, 1999).

Giannachi, Gabriella, Kaye, Nick, and Michael Shanks, eds., *Archaeologies of Presence: Art, Performance and the Persistence of Being* (London: Routledge, 2012).

Gill, Rosalind. *New Femininities: Postfeminism, Neoliberalism, and Subjectivity* (New York: Palgrave MacMillan, 2011).

Gillis, Stacy, Howie, Gillian, and Rebecca Munford. *Third Wave Feminism: A Critical Exploration* (New York: Palgrave Macmillan, 2007).

Gimlin, Debra. *Cosmetic Surgery Narratives: A Cross-Cultural Analysis of Women's Accounts* (New York: Palgrave McMillan, 2012).

Givner, Jessie. "Reproducing Reproductive Discourse: Optical Technologies in The Silent Scream and Eclipse of Reason," *Journal of Popular Culture* 28 (Winter 1994): 229–44.

Green, David, and Lowry, Joanna, eds., *Stillness and Time: Photography and the Moving Image* (Brighton: Photoforum and Photoworks, 2006).

Guthrie, Sharon R., and Castelnuovo, Shirley. "Elite Women Bodybuilders: Models of Resistance or Compliance?" *Play and Culture* 5 (1992): 401–8.

Halberstam, Judith. *Female Masculinity* (Durham: Duke University Press, 1988).

Hall, James. *Michelangelo and the Invention of the Human Body* (New York: Farrar, Straus and Giroux, 2005).

Hall, M. Ann. *Feminism and Sporting Bodies* (Champaign, IL: Human Kinetics, 1996).

Halperin, David M. *Saint Foucault: Towards a Gay Hagiography* (New York: Oxford University Press, 1995).

Harvey, David. *A Brief History of Neoliberalism* (Oxford: Oxford University Press, 2005).

Hayles, Katherine N. *How We Became Posthuman: Virtual Bodies in Cybernetics, Literature, and Informatics* (Chicago, IL: Chicago University Press, 1999).

Heinämaa, Sara. *Toward a Phenomenology of Sexual Difference: Husserl, Merleau-Ponty, Beauvoir* (Lanham, MD: Rowman and Littlefield Publishers, 2003).

Hewitt, Nancy A. *No Permanent Waves: Recasting Histories of U.S. Feminism* (New Brunswick, NJ: Rutgers University Press, 2010).

Heyes, Cressida J. *Self-Transformations: Foucault, Ethics, and Normalized Bodies* (Oxford: Oxford University Press, 2007).

Heyes, Cressida J., "Foucault Goes to Weight Watchers," *Hypatia* 21, 2 (Spring 2006): 126–49.

Heyes, Cressida J. and Jones, Meredith, eds. *Cosmetic Surgery: A Feminist Primer* (Aldershot: Ashgate, 2009).

Heywood, Leslie. *Bodymakers: A Cultural Anatomy of Women's Body Building* (New Brunswick, NJ: Rutgers University Press, 1998).

Heywood, Leslie. "Producing Girls: Empire, Sport, and the Neoliberal Body," in *Physical Culture, Power, and the Body*, eds. Jennifer Hargreaves and Patricia Vertinsky (New York: Routledge, 2007), 101–19.

Hoberman, John N. *Testosterone Dreams: Rejuvenation, Aphrodisia, Doping* (Berkeley, CA: University of California Press, 2005).

Holland, Samantha. *Pole Dancing, Empowerment, and Embodiment* (New York: Palgrave Macmillan, 2010).

Hollander, Anne. *Seeing Through Clothes* (Berkeley, CA: University of California Press, 1993).

Holmlund, Chris, "Visible Difference and Flex Appeal: The Body, Sex, Sexuality, and Race in the *Pumping Iron* Films," in *Building*

Bodies, ed. Pamela L. Moore (New Brunswick, NJ: Rutgers University Press, 1997), 87–102.

Hopkins, Burt C. *The Philosophy of Husserl* (Durham: Acumen, 2011).

Husserl, Edmund. "Perception, Spatiality, and the Body," in *The Essential Husserl: Basic Writings in Transcendental Phenomenology*, ed. Donn Welton (Bloomington, IN: Indiana University Press, 1999), 163–85.

Ian, Marcia. "From Abject to Object: Women's Bodybuilding," *Postmodern Culture* 1, 3 (May 1991): 1–10.

Ian, Marcia. "How Do You Wear Your Body? Bodybuilding and the Sublimity of Drag," in *Negotiating Lesbian and Gay Subjects*, eds. Monica Dorenkamp and Richard Henke (New York: Routledge, 1995), 71–92.

Ian, Marcia. "The Primitive Subject of Female Bodybuilding: Transgression and Other Postmodern Myths," *Differences: A Journal of Feminist Cultural Studies* 12, 3 (2001): 69–100.

Jackson, Mark. *Infanticide: Historical Perspectives on Child Murder and Concealment, 1550–2000* (Aldershot: Ashgate, 2002).

Jay, Martin. *Downcast Eyes: The Denigration of Vision in Twentieth-Century French Thought* (Berkeley, CA: University of California Press, 1993).

Jing-Bao, Nie. *Behind the Silence: Chinese Voices on Abortion* (New York: Rowman and Littlefield, 2005).

Jones, Amelia. *Body Art: Performing the Subject* (Minneapolis, MN: University of Minnesota Press, 1998).

Jones, Amelia. "Temporal Anxiety/'Presence' in *Absentia*: Experiencing Performance as Documentation," in *Archaeologies of Presence: Art, Performance and the Persistence of Being*, eds. Gabriella Giannachi, Nick Kaye, and Michael Shanks (London: Routledge, 2012), 197–221.

Jones, Amelia, and Heathfield, Adrian, eds., *Perform, Repeat, Record: Live Art in History* (Bristol: Intellect, 2012).

Jones, Stacy Holman. "Autoethnography: Making the Personal Political,' in *The Sage Handbook of Qualitative Research*, 3rd ed., eds. Norman K. Denzin and Yvonna S. Lincoln (Thousand Oaks, CA: Sage, 2005), 763–91.

Karjalainen, Pauli Tapani, and von Bonsdorff, Pauline. *Place and Embodiment* (Helsinki: University of Helsinki, 1995).

Karlyn, Kathleen Rowe. "Feminism in the Classroom: Teaching Towards the Third Wave," in *Feminism in Popular Culture*, eds. Joanne Hollows and Rachel Moseley (Oxford: Berg, 2006), 57–75.

Kaufman, Jason Edward. "Abramovic's School for Performance Art," *Art Newspaper* 16 (December 2007): 1.

Keenan, Catherine. "On the Relationship between Personal Photographs and Individual Memory," *History of Photography* 22, 1 (Spring 1998): 60–64.

Kennedy, Eileen, and Markula, Pirkko, eds. *Women and Exercise: The Body, Health and Consumerism* (New York: Routledge, 2011).

Klein, Alan M. *Little Big Men: Bodybuilding Subculture and Gender Construction* (Albany, NY: State University Press of New York, 1993).

Koekemoer, Dewaldt. "A Brief History of Figure Bodybuilding," *Ezine Articles* (1 October 2009): http://ezinearticles.com/?A-Brief-History-of-Figure-Bodybuilding&id=3017779 (accessed 26 October 2013).

Koster, Winny. *Secret Strategies: Women and Abortion in Yoruba Society, Nigeria* (Amsterdam: Aksant, 2003).

Krauss, Rosalind E. "Informe without Conclusion," *October* 78 (Fall 1996): 89–105.

Kristeva, Julia. *Powers of Horror: An Essay on Abjection*, trans. Leon S. Roudiez (New York: Columbia University Press, 1982).

Levin, Laura. "The Performative Force of Photography," *Photography and Culture* 2, 3 (November 2009): 327–36.

Longhurst, Robyn. "(Re)presenting Shopping Centres and Bodies: Questions of Pregnancy," in *New Frontiers of Space, Bodies and Gender*, ed. Rosa Ainley (London: Routledge, 1998), 20–34.

Longhurst, Robyn. *Maternities: Gender, Bodies and Space* (New York: Routledge, 2008).

Lowe, Maria R. *Women of Steel: Female Bodybuilders and the Struggle for Self-Definition* (New York: New York University Press, 1998).

Luft, Sebastian, and Overgaard, Soren. "Introduction" in *The Routledge Companion to Phenomenology*, eds. Sebastian Luft and Soren Overgaard (New York: Routledge, 2012), 1–15.

Mann, Patricia. *Micro-politics: Agency in a Post-Feminist Era* (Minneapolis, MN: University of Minnesota Press, 1994).

Mansfield, Alan, and McGinn, Barbara. "Pumping Irony: The Muscular and the Feminine," in *Body Matters: Essays on the Sociology of the Body*, eds. Sue Scott and David Morgan (London: Falmer Press, 1993), 49–68.

Markula, Pirkko. "Firm but Shapely, Fit but Sexy, Strong but Thin: The Postmodern Aerobicizing Female Bodies," *Sociology of Sport Journal*, 12 (1995): 424–53.

Markula, Pirkko. "Postmodern Aerobics," in *Athletic Intruders: Ethnographic Research on Women, Culture, and Exercise*, eds. Anne Bolin and Jane Granskog (Albany, NY: The State University of New York Press, 2003), 54–77.

Markula, Pirkko. *Foucault, Sport and Exercise: Power, Knowledge and Transforming the Self* (New York: Routledge, 2006).

Martin, Emily. *Flexible Bodies: Tracking Immunity in American Culture from the Days of Polio to the Age of AIDS* (Boston, MA: Beacon Press, 1994).

McEvilley, Thomas. *Art, Love, Friendship, Marina Abramovic and Ulay: Together and Apart* (New York: McPherson and Company, 2010).

McGrath, Shelly A., and Chananie-Hill, Ruth A. "'Big Freaky-Looking Women': Normalizing Gender Transgression Through Bodybuilding," *Sociology of Sport Journal* 26 (2009): 235–54.

McRobbie, Angela. *The Aftermath of Feminism: Gender, Culture, and Social Change* (London: Sage, 2009).

McTavish, Lianne. "Complicating Categories: Women, Gender and Sexuality in Seventeenth-Century French Visual Culture" (PhD dissertation, University of Rochester, 1996).

McTavish, Lianne. *Childbirth and the Display of Authority in Early Modern France* (Aldershot: Ashgate, 2005).

McTavish, Lianne. "Learning to See in New Brunswick, 1862–1929," *Canadian Historical Review* 87, 4 (December 2006): 553–81.

McTavish, Lianne. "The Cultural Production of Pregnancy: Bodies and Embodiment at a New Brunswick Abortion Clinic," *Topia: Canadian Journal of Cultural Studies* 20 (Fall 2008): 23–42.

McTavish, Lianne. "Reproduction and Regulation in Early Modern Europe," in *The Routledge History of Sex and the Body in the West, 1500 to the Present*, eds. Sarah Toulalan and Kate Fisher (New York: Routledge, 2013), 351–71.

Merleau-Ponty, Maurice. *Nature: Course Notes from the Collège de France*, trans. Robert Vallier, ed. Dominique Ségland (Evanston, IL: Northwestern University Press, 2003).

Moore, Pamela L., ed. *Building Bodies* (Newark, NJ: Rutgers University Press, 1997).

Morgan, Kathryn Pauly. "Women and the Knife: Cosmetic Surgery and the Colonization of Women's Bodies," *Hypatia* 6, 3 (Autumn 1991): 25–53

Morton-Brown, Marla. "Artificial Ef-femination: Female Bodybuilding and Gender Disruption," *Philosophy in the Contemporary World* 11, 1 (2004): 25–33.

Nast, Heidi J., and Steve Pile, eds. *Places Through the Body* (London: Routledge, 1998).

Obel, Camilla. "Collapsing Gender in Competitive Bodybuilding: Researching Contradiction and Ambiguity in Sport," in *Gender and Sport: A Reader*, eds. Sheila Scraton and Anne Flintoff (London: Routledge, 2002), 241–54.

Oksala, Johanna. "A Phenomenology of Gender," *Continental Philosophy Review* 39, 3 (2006): 229–44.

Olkowski, Dorothea, and Gail Weiss, eds. *Feminist Interpretations of Maurice Merleau-Ponty* (University Park, PA: The Pennsylvania State University Press, 2006).

Owen, Louise. "'Work that Body': Precarity and Femininity in the New Economy," *TDR: The Drama Review* 56, 4 (Winter 2012): 78–94.

Palley, Howard A., "Canadian Abortion Policy: National Policy and the Impact of Federalism and Political Implementation on Access to Services," *Publius: The Journal of Federalism* 36, 4 (2006): 565–86.

Parker, Rhian. *Women, Doctors and Cosmetic Surgery: Negotiating the "Normal" Body* (New York: Palgrave Macmillan, 2010).

Patton, Cindy. "'Rock Hard': Judging the Female Physique," *Journal of Sport and Social Issues* 25, 118 (2001): 118–40.

Peirce, Charles Sanders. *Peirce on Signs: Writings on Semiotics by Charles Sanders Peirce*, Ed. James Hoopes (Chapel Hill, NC: University of North Carolina Press, 1991).

Phelan, Peggy, ed. *Live Art in LA: Performance in Southern California, 1970–1983* (New York: Routledge, 2012).

Pijnappel, Johan. "Marina Abramovic, Reflections on the Mental Conditioning of the Artist," *Art and Design* 9 (September/October 1994): 48–55.

Pilcher, Jane. *Fifty Key Concepts in Gender Studies* (Thousand Oaks, CA: Sage, 2004).

Pitts-Taylor, Victoria. *Surgery Junkies: Wellness and Pathology in Cosmetic Culture* (New Brunswick, NJ: Rutgers University Press, 2007).

Pronger, Brian. *Body Fascism: Salvation in the Technology of Physical Fitness* (Toronto: University of Toronto Press, 1992).

Rebick, Judy. *Ten Thousand Roses: The Making of a Feminist Revolution* (Toronto: Penguin, 2005).

Richardson, Niall. "The Queer Activity of Extreme Male Bodybuilding: Gender Dissidence, Auto-eroticism and Hysteria," *Social Semiotics* 14, 1 (April 2004): 49–63.

Richardson, Niall. "Flex-rated! Female Bodybuilding: Feminist Resistance or Erotic Spectacle?" *Journal of Gender Studies* 17, 4 (December 2008): 289–301.

Richardson, Niall. *Transgressive Bodies: Representations in Film and Popular Culture* (Burlington, VT: Ashgate, 2010).

Richardson, Niall. "Introduction to Part 1: What is the 'Practice' of Bodybuilding?" in *Critical Readings in Bodybuilding*, eds. Adam Locks and Niall Richardson (New York: Routledge, 2012), 21–8.

Richmond, Susan N., "Sizing up the Dildo: Lynda Benglis' 1974 *Artforum* Advertisement as a Feminist Icon," *Paradoxa* 15 (2005): 24–34.

Rimke, Heidi. "Governing Citizens through Self-Help Literature," *Cultural Studies* 14, 1 (2000): 61–78.

Ritzer, George. *The McDonaldization of Society* (Thousand Oaks, CA: Sage, 2013).

Romdenh-Romluc, Komarine. "Maurice Merleau-Ponty," in *The Routledge Companion to Phenomenology*, eds. Sebastian Luft and Soren Overgaard (New York: Routledge, 2012), 103–12.

Rose, Gillian. *Visual Methodologies* (London: Sage, 2001).

Rothblum, Esther, and Solovay, Sandra, eds. *The Fat Studies Reader* (New York: New York University Press, 2009).

Roussel, Peggy, Griffet, Jean, and Pascal Duret. "The Decline of

Female Bodybuilding in France," *Sociology of Sport Journal* 20 (2003): 40–59.

Ryan, Jenny. "Muscling In: Gender and Physicality in Weight-training Culture," in *Reframing the Body*, ed. Nick Watson (New York: Palgrave, 2001), 166–86.

Saukko, Paula. *The Anorexic Self: A Personal, Political Analysis of Diagnostic Discourse* (Albany, NY: State University of New York Press, 2008).

Schippert, Claudia. "Can Muscles be Queer? Reconsidering the Transgressive Hyper-built Body," *Journal of Gender Studies* 16, 2 (July 2007): 155–71.

Sessions, Karen. *Figure Competition* (Karen Sessions Inc., 2010).

Shalma, Margaret. "Resistance Training: Re-Reading Fat Embodiment at a Women's Gym," *Disability Studies Quarterly* 28, 4 (Fall 2008): 1–10.

Silverman, Kaja. *Male Subjectivity at the Margins* (New York: Routledge, 1992).

Smith, Cherise. *Enacting Others: Politics of Identity in Eleanor Antin, Nikki S. Lee, Adrian Piper, and Anna Deavere Smith* (Durham, NC: Duke University Press, 2011).

Smith-Rosenberg, Carroll. "Constituting Nations/Violently Excluding Women: The First Contract with America," in *Virtual Gender: Fantasies of Subjectivity and Embodiment*, eds. Mary Ann O'Farrell and Lynne Vallone (Ann Arbor, MI: University of Michigan Press, 1999), 171–89.

Sontag, Susan. *On Photography* (New York: Farrar, Strauss, and Giroux, 1978).

Sparkes, Andrew C. "Autoethnography," *Telling Tales in Sport and Physical Activity: A Qualitative Journey* (Champaign, IL: Human Kinetics, 2002), 73–105.

St. Martin, Leena, and Gavey, Nicola. "Women's Bodybuilding: Feminist Resistance and/or Femininity's Recuperation?" *Body and Society* 2 (1996): 45–57.

Steinmetz, Julia, Cassils, Heather, and Clover Leary. "Behind Enemy Lines: Toxic Titties Infiltrate Vanessa Beecroft," *Signs: Journal of Women in Culture and Society* (Spring 2003): 753–83.

Stiles, Kristine, Biesenbach, Klaus, and Chrissie Iles. *Marina Abramović* (London: Phaidon, 2008).

Strauss, Sarah. *Positioning Yoga: Balancing Acts Across Cultures* (Oxford: Berg, 2005).

Stoller, Silvia. "Reflections on Feminist Merleau-Ponty Skepticism," *Hypatia* 15, 1 (Winter 2000): 175–82.

Stryker, Susan, and Whittle, Stephen, eds. *The Transgender Studies Reader* (New York: Routledge, 2006).

Tagg, John. *The Burden of Representation: Essays on Photographies and Histories* (Amherst, MA: University of Massachusetts Press, 1988).

Tagg, John. *The Disciplinary Frame: Photographic Truths and the Capture of Meaning* (Minneapolis, MN: University of Minnesota Press, 2009).

Tillmann-Healy, Lisa. "A Secret Life in a Culture of Thinness: Reflections on Body, Food, and Bulimia," in *Composing Ethnography: Alternative Forms of Qualitative Writing*, eds. C. Ellis and A. P. Bochner (Walnut Creek, CA: Altamira Press, 1996), 76–108.

Tillmann, Lisa. "Body and Bulimia Revisited: Reflections on 'A Secret Life'," *Journal of Applied Communication Research* 37, 1 (February 2009): 98–112.

Todd, Dennis. *Imagining Monsters: Miscreations of the Self in Eighteenth-Century England* (Chicago, IL: University of Chicago Press, 1995).

Ulrich-Obrist, Hans. *Marina Abramović* (Cologne: W. König, 2010).

Vinegar, Aron. *I am a Monument: On Learning from Las Vegas* (Cambridge, MA: MIT Press, 2008).

Wang, Eugene. "Watching the Steps: Peripatetic Vision in Medieval China," in *Visuality Before and Beyond the Renaissance: Seeing as Others Saw*, ed. Robert S. Nelson (Cambridge: Cambridge University Press, 1997), 116–42.

Watson, Elwood, and Darcy Martin, eds. *"There She Is, Miss America": The Politics of Sex, Beauty, and Race in America's Most Famous Pageant* (New York: Palgrave MacMillan, 2004).

Westcott, James. *When Marina Abramović Dies: A Biography* (Cambridge, MA: MIT Press, 2010).

Williamson, Lola. *Transcendent in America: Hindu-Inspired Meditation Movements as New Religion* (New York: New York University Press, 2010).

Wolf, Naomi. *The Beauty Myth: How Images of Beauty are Used Against Women* (Toronto: Random House, 1990).

Woods-Marsden, Joanna. *Renaissance Self-Portraiture: The Visual*

Construction of Identity and Social Status of the Artist (New Haven, CT: Yale University Press, 1998).

Young, Iris Marion. *Throwing Like a Girl and Other Essays in Feminist Philosophy and Social Theory*, (Bloomington, IN: Indiana University Press, 1990).

Index